Unrave Mysteries of Hinduism

Umasankar Raja

Copyright

ISBN: 978-3-00-067577-5

Acknowledgements

I would like to dedicate this book to all the enlightened masters who have spent their whole life in conveying the truth to the masses and helped them to realize the life which is beyond all dimensions. In spite of their effort in conveying the truth for thousands of years, still there exists majority of population who are living in ignorance. This book will unravel the mysteries in Hinduism and fill the gap, which the awakened beings wanted to do, in order to awake the humanity from the dream they were dreaming since long and bring them to reality.

Special thanks to my wife Siva Priya for her continuous support and valuable suggestions right from the initial conception, until the final publication of the manuscript.

Preface

This book was written with an intention to convey the message which has been revealed to me by the existence otherwise with my limited intelligence it is impossible for me to arrive here. Even if one spends his whole life in reading all the religious literature, one may not be able to find the details which are explained in this book. This book is full of surprises because the truth has been hidden for the last 25 centuries and people have been conditioned to believe in something which is not true. This book will give the clear picture of what Hinduism mean and explain the concept of god in Hinduism. Most of the unanswered questions are explained with proper scientific facts. This book will re-establish the order in Hinduism which has been lost and misused by various religious sects within Hinduism for their personal interest. Also I want to remind you that it is impossible to realize god or attain enlightenment by reading this book because Enlightenment is not about becoming someone, rather it's about attaining one's original nature which one has lost after acquiring knowledge. In fact the whole purpose of this book is to make it clear that God can't be confined into any book because you are part of existence and god is in your own nature which you will understand after reading this book.

Author can be reached through **www.knowerandknown.org**

Table of Contents

Table of Contents (Cont.)

List of Illustrations

List of Illustrations (Cont.)

List of Illustrations (Cont.)

1 Introduction

I am Umasankar Raja. I come from a small town named Ramanathapuram, located in south of Tamil Nadu in India. I belong to a traditional Hindu family with firm beliefs in Hinduism. Right from my childhood, I have lived in a joint family together with my father's three brothers and grandparents. Ours is a middle class family with limited wealth which was good enough to support the family's basic needs. My Grandfather was a firm devotee of God Shiva (God of destroyer as per Hinduism). He always used to share so many miracles which had happened in his life because of his faith in god Shiva. In fact he is the one who has named me as Umasankar which literally means Uma (Parvathi, Shiva's wife) and Sankar (Shiva). He insisted me to worship and believe in Shiva, so naturally I also developed strong faith in god Shiva. I used to pray to every god in Hinduism even though our family god is Karthikeya (the younger son of Lord Shiva) but Shiva is the one, who is close to my heart. As there are so many gods in Hinduism, every Hindu family will have a family god, whom they consider as their ancestors and worship them. I respected all the religious traditions even though I didn't know the meaning behind most of the things we followed. Sometimes I even thought that Hinduism is the only true religion.

When I reached my teen age, my search for deeper meaning of life started growing. Most of the time, I used to go to the Shiva temple in our town and spend time alone. During that time, one of my uncles who was a follower of swami Vivekananda has given me a small book about Vivekananda and told me to read it. Swami Vivekananda was very well known throughout India because of his famous speech about Hinduism at World's Parliament of Religions which had happened in Chicago in 1893. I have read that book which describes his life history and his ideas about life in brief. He didn't talk much about God but mostly about one's inner potential to achieve anything which one wants. Two of his famous quotes which I always remember are "***Strength is life and weakness is death***" and "***Arise and Awake***". At that time, I didn't know what does it really mean.

I was very good at studies and scored good marks in higher secondary and opted to study Production Engineering in a college in Chennai. I did my graduation with good grades and appeared for GATE exam, an exam to qualify for higher studies in India. I failed to qualify the exam in my first attempt by a narrow margin, but I was confident that it is possible to crack it if approached properly. So I decided to dedicate a year for preparation and collected all the required materials and prepared myself at my home. During this time I had gone through severe psychological pressure because in India you are not allowed to do anything which is out of the box. The moment one finishes his graduation he should directly land in a job. If someone deviates from this pattern then he will be considered as useless. That's how my friends and relatives had seen me as if I was wasting my time during that period. Every day one or the other gave me tonnes of suggestions. Even when I tried to explain what I was doing, they were unable to understand. So I stopped answering them and focused fully on my preparation. I used to spent 16 hours a day for preparation, because of my hard work I had cleared it and got admission for M.Tech in Production Engineering in IIT Delhi which is one of the top ranked institutes in India and well known around the world. During my last semester, I secured a job in one of the leading German automobile manufacturer. I was placed in their research and development center located in Bangalore. I moved to Bangalore and started my career. I lived with two of my friends in an apartment for almost 2 years and later they moved to different apartment when they got married. Initially I felt lonely but later I started liking it. I liked the freedom of not depending on anyone for anything. I realized that I have much time after office hours so I started reading books. I started with "My Experiments with Truth" by Mahatma Gandhi and some other biographies and then I slowly moved to philosophy and history. I read so many books on philosophy and finally narrowed down to particular author Osho. He didn't write any books but his talks were recorded and later published as books. I was amazed how a person has such profound knowledge on everything. He was a spiritual guru but he talked about some of the most forbidden topics in India especially about sex. After reading his talks on sex, I realized that sex is not a taboo as described by religions rather it is a natural human instinct which can be transcended if one lives with complete awareness. I found him very interesting; his works on Zen has impressed me a lot.

Every day I used to read few pages of his books and shared it with my colleagues at office. They all started thinking that I am a spiritual person and sometimes even people used to have a conversation with me to get relaxed. But I was just sharing the knowledge which I had read in his books. This has slowly taken me out of traditional conditioning. Earlier I was bound to believe that as per Indian traditions, one must get married to a person chosen by their parents. So I had never looked for a girl whole heartedly and left that job to my parents, because in India still there is a wide spread projection that if a man chooses his girl, then his parents has not brought him up properly.

Meanwhile I started travelling to Germany for business reasons. As I worked for R&D division, it is important to interact with customers face to face in order to understand their requirements and to make communication better. I used to travel twice for a period of six weeks each in first half and second half of the year. First time when I visited, I didn't like it much because my apartment was located in a remote place near to the production facility. Streets were very silent and there were only few people on the streets as well as in my apartment. Another reason might be I was not fluent in German. So I didn't interact much with others at office, except my customer. It was a kind of different atmosphere for an Indian who has spent his whole life in crowd and noise. I like being alone but that was a totally different kind of loneliness, where I felt like an alien in unknown world. But from my second visit, I started liking it because it has given me a big break from noisy and polluted Bangalore. I started enjoying silence. There was a forest nearby my apartment, where I used to go alone and sometimes even in the nights and forget myself by observing the sky and stars. Those were the moments in my life when I understood that there is a deeper connection between mankind and nature.

I was eagerly waiting as well as excited about my next travel and carried so many books to read over the weekends. Being a Hindu I had never tasted pork in India but I have come out of that conditioning and enjoyed the life as the way it is. I started tasting German beers and their traditional dishes like schnitzel, currywurst and bratwurst. It became clear to me that people here have developed different kind of life style and food habits as per their climatic conditions. I liked their work-life balance and the silence which prevailed there. I decided to apply for jobs in Germany and attended couple of interviews but it didn't work. In fact when I was alone in nature, I prayed to it, to bring me here not with an intention to earn more money but to be one with it.

Back in India when I started opening my heart, I found my life partner who was sitting next to me in my office. Both of us started as friends and gradually love has blossomed between us. A year later, she got a job offer in Chennai, so I also resigned my job and moved to Chennai to work in another US based automobile manufacturer. Meanwhile I kept searching for job in Germany and also motivated her to apply there. We both applied for almost one and half year but there were no favourable response so we decided to settle down in Chennai and stopped applying further. Miraculously she got a call from a company which she has applied long back and everything went well and they offered her a job in a company located in Bayern, Germany.

With great difficulty we got permission from our parents for marriage because we are from different Indian states where they speak totally different language. My parents were so much concerned that they cannot communicate with their In-laws.

Later she resigned her job in Chennai and went to Germany and after 6 months I also resigned my job and joined with her without any job offer. I was very confident that I have a world class master's degree, German language skills and work experience in leading automobile manufacturers, so without a second thought I landed in Germany. We started living in Traunstein, a beautiful town situated on the border of Germany and Austria. I was happy that nature has heard my prayers and brought me here.

I started applying for jobs in Munich and nearby locations around our region. As I worked in Research department, my entire work experience was focused on a very narrow topic. So I would fit only into the organisations which were working on that topic. I applied to an automobile major head quartered in Munich. But my application had been kept under scrutiny for long time. I was not able to find any suitable position in the companies near to my locality. Everyone conducted interview but finally they chose someone else. I also applied to the company where my wife works but it didn't work.

My wife used to go to office early in the morning and return in the evening around 4pm. I kept applying for various companies throughout the day and will be waiting for my wife to reach home. I have written 100's of applications with cover letter to show my willingness to work on any topic outside of my expertise. After few weeks it became clear to me that to find a job I must relocate to some other region in Germany. But my wife felt comfortable working with her current company and we didn't want to miss each other by working at different places. So I skipped the idea of relocating and kept applying without giving up.

Meanwhile there was a huge pressure from my parents in India. They were not happy that I had left a job in renowned organisation and came to Germany without an offer. Almost every week they started enquiring the progress and kept blaming me for leaving the job in India. Basically in India, people worry too much about their surroundings than themselves. Every decision will be influenced by others. My parents were not able to answer some relatives who started torturing them with all unnecessary questions about my job. I felt it's too much to continue with this unwanted pressure. We thought that first we must calm down their minds and take their worries away by giving them false information. So we decided and informed my parents that I got a job near to my wife's workplace. As expected it worked well and they stopped asking about job and we also felt little relived. But three months has passed without any positive results.

I applied for another three months but the situation didn't change. I thought I should refrain sometime from applying further because it was really frustrating to see 100's of my application getting rejected. Since long I also badly wanted to take a break because being the elder son of the family, I have gone through so much of pressure to fulfil my family obligations. I was always considering the idea of taking a break for sometime once my sisters get married. Many times I had a thought that Why am I continuously running? Is there any purpose in this running, why I need to stick to this particular pattern of education, work, family and retirement? While preparing for my masters I have understood that taking a diversion from routine will make lots of difference. So I decided to stop job hunting and take a break for sometime without worrying about anything in order to relax and understand what I really wanted to do? I shared this idea with my wife, as she was confident of handling our financials with single income; she encouraged me to do what I wanted.

"Life spent on imitating and following others can't be called as life rather a lie"

2 Period of Depression

I stopped applying for jobs and started relaxing, for almost two months I haven't done anything. I simply stayed at home and used to go to forest and walk along the river side and spent most of the time alone. I started getting so many philosophical thoughts during this time, so I always carried a notebook with me and started writing whatever comes to my mind. I thought that nature has given me an opportunity to explore and understand what I really want to do. Also since long I wanted to write a book about my Grandpa so I started writing.

Back in India, my father who was in his early sixties suddenly had a chest pain and was admitted at a local hospital, after angiogram examination doctor confirmed that he has two blocks in his heart which need to be cleared immediately. So he has been taken to a hospital in Madurai (a city located 110 km away from my town) for operation. My sister called me and told to arrange an amount which was really big for me at that time. On one hand, I was not able to believe that how it has happened to my father, who exercises regularly and maintains fitness, in fact he doesn't look like a man of 60's. On other hand, I was worried about how to arrange the money for operation. I conveyed the situation to my wife, without a second thought, she transferred the required amount. I was so happy that my wife understood my situation but at the same time I started feeling low for passing my burden on her shoulders. It was so depressing for me. In the mean time, my father got operated and doctors had cleared the blocks and placed two stents (to improve blood flow) in his heart. He was kept under observation for few days and sent back home.

This incident has suddenly lowered my self esteem for depending on my wife for my survival even though she has never given any chance for such thoughts. It started hurting my ego and my mind started generating so many unwanted negative thoughts. I felt like I am lost and I started feeling lonely. Most of the time, I was hiding inside the home to avoid facing neighbours and their unnecessary questions about my employment. Also Germany's cold and dark winter without sunlight had worsened the feeling of depression further. As I stopped interacting with people, slowly I lost the grip on German language and was not able to speak even basic German. I stopped speaking with my friends and temporarily suspended all my social media applications.

Every now and then I used to go to Traunstein railway station to receive my wife back from work. While walking towards the station, I felt like that the whole world is against me and it's a dangerous place where I can't survive. I was unable to walk with so much of burden in my heart. I kept repeating the statement that 'this situation will change' like a mantra and reach the station. I felt a temporary relief from the pressure which I was carrying, when I see my wife at the station. But I didn't share about my psychological condition which I thought may upset her. Out of my frustration, sometimes I even shouted on her without any reason and later asked sorry for that.

There arrived a good news, my wife got pregnant. We were happy that a new member is coming and going to brighten up our life. At the same time there was a slight worry because she must take rest during her pregnancy which raises the question of how we could be able to manage the expenses during that time. But we found that Germany has good social security benefits for pregnant women. There is a law which protects the job of women employees during maternity, also provides financial assistance for a certain period after child's birth. We were at peace for sometime then another unpleasant incident happened, in the 8th week of pregnancy my wife had a bleeding. We consulted doctor and based on his suggestion, she took medication for a month and went on complete bed rest. I have taken care of all the household activities completely during this period. We took every possible measure to save the child, but it didn't bear the fruit, she had a miscarriage and we lost our baby. This incident had made our life even worse. She couldn't bear the loss and has cried for so many days. I tried to console her by saying, may be the soul doesn't want to suffer by taking birth that's why it has left us very early. She replied then why it has to come in the first place. I was left with no answer.

We conveyed about this tragedy to our parents. Everyone gave their bit of consolation and told to take care of health. My wife was not able to come out of this situation for few months. She used to tell me, may be the soul doesn't want us to be its parents. Couldn't we be good parents? Everyone around us was happily getting married and becoming parents but why we have to struggle so much for everything. What's the reason behind this entire struggle? Did we commit so many sins in our past life and that's why we are facing the consequences in this life. How long we should keep struggling? She said that, she couldn't suffer anymore, enough of suffering and she broke in tears. Even though I wanted to cry, I didn't cry in front of her which I thought will deepen her sorrows. I used to convince her that next time everything will be fine, may be the fetus didn't form properly. It's not our fault and we don't need to take any blame for this.

I was so much upset with my life. I started asking myself is this why I have come to Germany, to struggle for everything? I went to the forest and sat there in silence and asked nature 'why did you bring me here?' I accept the fact that I wanted to be with you but with so much of suffering and pain I couldn't feel the peace which I experienced earlier. I cried out loud for some time, later came back home with a temporary relief. As we were too much pressurised, we badly needed a break from our routine. So we decided to go for a vacation to come out of the stressful situation and to forget the tragedies happened. For the next one month we were busy in preparing for the trip. We planned a weeklong trip to nearby countries. We visited Budapest, Bratislava, Warsaw and Prague. We enjoyed the trip; there we got some positive outlook of life which was much needed for us.

A month later we travelled to India and visited our parents and relatives. We made a family trip to some of the oldest and well known temples which are located close to my home town. Luckily our visit coincided with the Thaipoosam (a festival majorly celebrated in Tamil Nadu in the Tamil month of Thai (Jan/February)). Even though this festival is traditionally celebrated in all god Karthikeya (Murugan) temples in Tamil Nadu, a totally different kind of celebration happens in a place called Vadalur, where my younger sister has settled after marriage. Only during this time the sanctum of "Hall of True knowledge" consecrated by 19th century Tamil saint and poet called Vallalar remains open. People generally call it as Vallalar temple but we couldn't find any god deity like in other traditional Hindu temples rather there is a flame which was said to be lit by him. He said that God is a divine flame and the same flame has manifested as soul inside everyone and there are seven veils which are covering this soul. By removing these seven layers one can attain Moksha (liberation) and become immortal. He had conveyed this truth in the 'Hall of True Knowledge' to everyone during the Thaipoosam festival by unveiling the 7 layers of screens and finally showing the lamp to symbolically represent the divine nature of soul and Self-realization. This practise has been followed even after his disappearance for past 150 years. As my sister invited us for this celebration, we got a chance to witness the divine flame lit by him.

We came back from India and started our life with fresh energy. I continued writing the book about my Grandpa. Few weeks I remained positive but again the feeling of worthlessness returned. I got stuck; I was not able to write anything. My mind started recollecting all the past incidents and made me to believe that I am incompetent and I am a failure. It took me into a state of deep depression and I started feeling that I am good for nothing. My self esteem has gone down; future looked gloomy without any ray of hope. I was not able to sleep at nights. I got so many unwanted intimidating dreams which projected me as a loser. I was fuming inside but I didn't share it with my wife. I started hating the world of comparison, where everyone is compared with others for everything. It's been almost a year and half, I am still dependent on my wife for which I was ashamed of. Before that I was considered as an example for pursuing one's passion and making successful career in it but now I am absolutely zero. My mind started generating all unnecessary thoughts by comparing myself with all my friends and relatives. Everyone looked happy and wealthy except me. Everyone has settled well except me. I started imagining that if my friends and relatives come to know about my current situation then they will definitely consider me as an absolute loser in life. I always had an opinion that I am very intelligent, being educated from world-class institutes and worked for world-class companies, I thought I have the capability to crack anything without much effort but life has proved me wrong. It shattered my self-image and made me realise that 'I know nothing'. Usually I don't like comparison, but I was not able to stop this unwanted thoughts arising out of my mind. Except my in-laws, no one knows that I was idle; soon they also started enquiring about what I am going to do? But my wife being a strong lady didn't give much room for her parents to know more about what's happening with our life. She simply closed the conversation by saying that we are doing good and they don't need to worry about us now and also in future, we will take care of ourselves.

I was feeling very low for not being able to fulfil my family's expectations and their trust on me. Whole day I was struggling to control these unwanted thoughts, they started consuming my day and night. To divert these thoughts I used to watch movies one after another continuously without giving any break because if I give a break again these thoughts started torturing me. I started becoming aggressive and angry on me as well as to my wife. My one and only question was "why life seems very difficult to live, can't we survive peacefully without much struggle?" Anger, jealously, hatred had become part of me. But I have hidden everything with a fake smile. Few months have passed just like that, then I realised that I need to control this unwanted negative thoughts which were making me more stressful. I read some books about positive thinking and pasted some motivational quotes on the walls around to stay positive.

Even though I like being in nature, I stopped going to the forest and river near my home because I was not in a state to enjoy anything. I was continuously thinking about future. Thoughts were very repetitive. Mind projected the same thoughts again and again and again. But I was not able to stop it and immersed myself in believing those negative thoughts as reality. I was not able to do anything. Even to go for shopping to nearby supermarket seemed like a big task for me. Thoughts were so heavy, it has almost occupied me. I started noticing so many grey hairs suddenly even in my moustache. One thing became clear that I must do something to stop these thoughts otherwise I may end up my life.

To get rid of these thoughts I started consoling myself by saying that "I have come here to enjoy nature but after coming, my priorities have changed. Instead of enjoying nature, I started worrying by locking myself inside four concrete walls. Let's go out and live now instead of worrying about future". I understood that I am creating my own hell by living in future uncertainties. Then I started going to a viewpoint behind the hospital nearby my home and watch the snow covered mountains and try to lose myself in that beauty. One day I asked nature "ok I don't want anything more than being with you, I am happy without anything but my wife wants a child. Please give us a child, we will take care and will raise the child with an awareness that humans are part of you and we are coming from you".

I was fighting and trying to win the battle against my own mind. But every time it has won. I started watching so many videos about psychology and positive thinking every day. In some videos they spoke about meditation and mind control are key things to be successful in life. Since long my wife was also insisting me to practise meditation, to get refresh internally and to create a positive vibration. So I decided to practise meditation in order to get out of my never ending thoughts which were consuming my whole life energy.

"In the name of survival man has been taught to carry the unnecessary burden of the mind and it's never ending thinking and so the suffering".

3 Meditation

I regularly spend 30 minutes a day for yoga or exercise, I thought of including meditation to this routine. Again there was a confusion on what kind of meditation to do because there are so many meditation techniques like concentrating on certain objects or on one's own breath and also there are different types of mantra meditation. But since I have read in many Osho's books, he always suggested relaxing instead of focusing or concentrating on certain things. He says "relaxing into one's inner being is basically meditation". So I also decided to sit silently and relax totally without any motive or objective to be achieved through it.

Initially I tried to sit silently for sometime but I was unable to sit even for 5 minutes. There were so many thoughts which I found were more disturbing while practising meditation than in normal time. Maybe it happens in the initial stage of practising meditation, the more one tries to get rid of thoughts, the more one will get pulled by the thoughts. As I sat for meditation immediately after workouts naturally my focus was on my body and breath, so I just started observing my body and breath for sometime and it has given me good relief. I was able to stop thinking for sometime but I felt little back pain. So to avoid back pain, I used to lay down on the yoga mat and most of the time I slept off.

Few weeks have passed the quality of meditation as well as the duration has increased gradually and it gave me the relaxation which I badly wanted. I totally let go off my fear. I shared with my wife that I was feeling better after including meditation in my daily routine. Situation seemed to be in control and life started getting better. It became clear to me that I perceive the world around through my mind and if I can keep my mind positive then the world around also looks promising.

Meanwhile my wife got pregnant, we were happy but at the same time slightly afraid because of the last unpleasant incident. I convinced her by saying that everything will be fine this time, nature will take care, we don't need to worry. We decided not to share about her pregnancy to anyone, not even to our parents. Once everything goes well then we thought of sharing it after sixth month of pregnancy. But happiness is always short lived; it never lasted for more than few weeks. Again exactly in the 8th week of her pregnancy, she had a bleeding. This time it was so severe and with so much of cramps. By looking at it, she confirmed that our baby has gone again because we experienced this situation before. Neither she cried nor me. That's what happens when you were struck with disaster again and again. We have become strong and felt that if this is the way it has to happen then let it happen. What we could do when the situation is beyond our control other than accepting it. But I had a gut feeling that baby is still safe in her womb. I told her not to worry, let's go to the hospital and confirm before coming to any conclusion by ourselves. We took an emergency appointment and reached clinic. Doctor has examined using the ultrasound and confirmed that the baby is safe; also he has shown us the heart beat and baby moving inside the womb. We almost cried there out of happiness. Just within hours we have seen the hell of our life and came back to normal. Doctor told us to take a bed rest for few weeks and has given sickness certificate to submit to her company. We were happy and we decided not to risk our baby's life at any cost. We thought of taking leaves until she recovers completely. We were not ready to bear the pain again. Also my wife's colleague explained her about a law in Germany which allows pregnant woman to take leave until maternity in case of any serious health issues.

She took 2 more weeks leave, after that we consulted doctor, he suggested going for a long leave till maternity and has given 'Beschaftigungsverbot' (not allowed to work certificate for women employees, especially when there is a risk of health and life involved). We submitted the copy of certificate to her company and to the insurance so that they will take care of the monthly expenses until maternity. She took complete bed rest for almost two months after that her health started improving. She gradually came out of fear and started walking slowly. During this period I was taking care of all household activities but continued meditating regularly.

She always wanted me to be with her. For some weeks we were watching so many travel based movies as both of us like travelling. We have covered almost all the travel genre movies during that period in almost all the languages. We went for regular checkups and the baby was growing as per the week's calculations and slowly we were coming out of the fear.

One day in the evening, I sat for meditation as usual. I received an energy with so much of intensity which I can't imagine or explain in words. "Even though language has an inherent limitation when it comes to expressing the experience, I have tried my best to convey it". The energy was so intense that out of fear I thought of opening the eyes but I decided to experience it without any interruptions. I felt like as if my head is literally spinning and the rotation is spreading to other parts of the body. It was very continuous with loads of energy striking me again and again like lighting. I completely forgot where I am and in which position I was sitting. I felt like my head has turned back. The energy was so heavy that I felt my body was unable to take such an amount of energy. It has taken me into a different state of experience, where my physical body has completely dissolved. This experience has lasted for sometime and then the intensity of the energy gradually reduced. After that there arrived a state of peace, stillness, silence which I have never experienced. I could feel that something which is totally unknown is happening to me. I remained in that position for sometime without opening my eyes. I sat for more than one and half hour which was very surprising, as usually I sit for not more than 30 minutes for meditation. This experience of silence was pure, absolute and it has totally absorbed me. Later when I opened my eyes, there were no thoughts and I could feel that stillness for the rest of the day.

Meanwhile my wife not hearing anything from me for quite some time came to the room where I was meditating to confirm that everything is fine. I told her that I have experienced something totally strange today. I had the glimpses of inner peace, which in India people call it as Samadhi (state of oneness). I can't explain it in words but it was so calm and serene. All the yogis who were talking about inner peace were actually true. Inside us, there is something which is greater than our body and mind and that can be experienced in deep silence it seems.

After this experience, I stopped reading books which I thought will create an unnecessary expectations and imaginations on something which is happening on its own. Earlier I used to drink beer every weekend to get rid of the negative thoughts temporarily but I stopped drinking beer, because it's clear that the happiness and peacefulness which I experienced from that energy was incomparable to anything which a man can get from any worldly things. It became clear to me that something new is happening to me and I must respect it and ready to accept it.

I started meditating for longer duration with an expectation to receive that energy and happiness again. I started craving for that state of inner peace. It seemed to me that I was chasing it and sometimes get frustrated after trying so hard. I tried different techniques to artificially bring that peace by focusing my attention on breath and on the center of eyebrows. I tried all methods but nothing worked, so I have given up considering it as an accident and continued with meditation normally.

I also advised my wife to join me for meditation. She has already practised meditation some years ago but has given up as she didn't feel any difference. But after hearing my personal experience, she decided to meditate again. Anyway meditation is good for health, particularly during pregnancy. We both sat for meditation every evening without fail.

In the beginning I told her to sit silent, don't think about anything, just observe your thoughts and relax. Even if thought comes, don't get associated with it rather try to watch it. Initially she was not able to sit even for 10 minutes and complained about her back pain and feeling sleepy. I told her that all these things happened to me in the beginning, don't stop it just continue it without any expectations. Few weeks have passed, we both were regularly meditating in the evening and slowly she also sat with me for longer duration. In fact we stopped noticing the time.

Few days later, I experienced that energy again. It was so intense as if an elephant is trying to sit on me. But I just let it happen instead of trying to stop it out of fear. Again loads of energy struck me and took me to somewhere; I totally dissolved in it and was taken into pure silence (state of oneness). Everything stopped in that stillness. After an hour I opened my eyes and told to my wife that I have experienced that energy again. I was feeling so much silence inside which I couldn't explain. She asked me, why it is not happening to her. I told her that, perhaps she needs some more time to let go her thoughts and to relax completely. I was also chasing for this experience for quite some time but it didn't happen. But when I relaxed totally without craving for anything it has happened. It seems like we just need to relax, it will happen when we are ready and totally empty of our thoughts. Even after that incident, I was just normal and my life was going as usual. I continued writing book in the morning and meditated in the evening. There were ups and downs in life but it didn't affect me much. My life started changing inwardly rather than outwardly. We both started feeling calmness and accepted the life the way it is. While cooking and during dinner we were discussing about the changes which we notice in each other. There were no fights between us which used to happen earlier for very small reasons. Life started showering love on us, we started enjoying every small thing and were happy and content with our life. We were so concerned about our spending earlier now we realised that we don't need to fear so much about the future and it is important to enjoy every moment. We started going to restaurants regularly. We have visited different restaurants and tasted different varieties of food in and around Traunstein. We stopped discussing about unnecessary things about our relatives and friends, which were not at all helpful in anyway. All kinds of comparison had vanished. We even stopped watching movies because in most of the movies they show unimaginable and unrealistic things which we felt were simply waste of time and causes unnecessary mental disturbance. We were leading a simple but most satisfied and happy life.

"When one stops worrying about the future and regretting about the past, then one starts living in the present which is actually life".

4 Ego to Eternity

Few days later I experienced the same energy again in the middle of the night. I was lying in the bed and it was not a dream for sure, all the experiences happened again. Next day morning I woke up and went for jogging as usual at 5 am which is usually dark in Germany, so I was focusing on the foot path, taking care of every step. I felt something has changed in me but not sure what it was. I came back home, got refreshed and switched on my laptop to review what I have written so far. I was looking at the monitor but I observed a change in my vision. It seems like someone inside me was looking through me with so much of silence. I felt absolute peace, no thoughts, no confusion and no anxiety but it was totally strange. I started hearing a continuous noise which I thought was coming from my old laptop. It was so disturbing that I took a pair of cotton balls and placed in both of my ears. But still I was able to hear that noise. I thought may be its time to replace my old laptop which was making much noise in the name of functioning.

I wanted to close the laptop as soon as possible to get rid of this noise. Meanwhile I finished my breakfast, switched off my laptop and turned off the monitor. Surprisingly even after shutting down the laptop, I was hearing that noise. It was continuous without any gap. I thought maybe I have a problem with my ears because of too much of exposure to laptop's noise. I shared this problem with my wife that I am hearing a continuous noise in my ear even after switching off the laptop. She also suggested changing the laptop, as anyway we need a better and faster performing one. I convinced her by saying let's see for a couple of months, if it continues to generate noise like this then we will consider changing it. I thought maybe I had an illusion of hearing the noise even after closing the laptop.

I was hearing the sound whole day, I went for a walk in the evening and I felt something is missing in me. I was feeling very light and joyful but I was not able to spot the difference exactly what was missing. It seemed like something has happened to my eyes because my vision has become very clear. I thought maybe there is some problem in my brain because of which I am feeling the effect on senses, initially on ears and now on eyes. I didn't tell anything about the change in my vision to my wife. I didn't want to scare her by telling about all these things. But I was internally very happy, there were no disturbances inside, it was crystal clear without any thoughts.

Evening we sat for meditation as usual. Immediately after closing my eyes, I was into total silence but this time I didn't receive any energy like before. It was serene silence, so intense that I totally forgot my body. We finished after an hour and when I opened my eyes I was in the same experience. It was absolute silence. I was looking at a water mug kept on the table in front of me, it seemed like I am watching myself. After finishing my dinner, I sat again and observed the objects around me. I was totally in present moment with complete awareness, without even a single thought. I kept watching the things around me like a kid without any idea about the world.

I was not able to differentiate between myself and the surroundings. I was not able to identify exactly where my body ends and where the existence begins. I felt like that my energy has expanded and filled the entire room. I was able to experience the continuity in the space and the objects in the room are distorting the space. Perfect example could be, when you go for scuba diving, you can feel that you are within the water as well you can observe that all the aquatic creatures and planktons are distorting the water. It was a unique experience which I ever had in my life until that time. I was still doubtful and thought maybe I was focusing too much under the warm white light of the room because of which my sense of perception appeared differently. Whatever the reason might be, I didn't want to get up from the place where I was sitting but it was already late so I went to bed, but I was hearing the sound continuously without break and slept with some difficulty.

Next morning when I woke up and went to bathroom to get refresh, I observed the same freshness all over the objects and was happy about the changes happening in me. I went for jogging and came back and switched on the laptop. When the laptop started, it again created the noise but when I observed closely that the noise which I was hearing whole day was totally different from the one which was coming from the laptop. There was a clear difference between both the sounds and I was hearing both of them simultaneously. I paid close attention and differentiated that I was hearing the laptop noise through the ears but the other sound I was hearing through somewhere on the left side of the head, above the ear. I moved away from the laptop and noticed that the laptop noise was decreasing but the other sound has been received with same intensity irrespective of wherever I moved. I doubted, maybe it's a kind of divine sound. I have read so many books about religion and philosophy, but nowhere have I read anything about this kind of sound. In Hinduism they used to say that the universe was made up of sound and it's the source of everything. It's the sound of OM (sound of creation). But the sound which I was hearing is not exactly OM. I tried to listen to it to check whether it is a kind of language to be understood. It was not an understandable sound at all but continuous without beginning and ending.

I started doubting myself and wondered how a common man like me could be able to hear such a divine sound which yogis and mystics have heard after years of practising meditation and austerity. But by observing all the changes happened to me over the past few days I thought maybe I have attained enlightenment? It means an unexpected and unimaginable thing has happened to me because from my childhood I have heard only very few people have attained enlightenment and it is the ultimate thing that can happen to a man in his life. I was hesitant to even share it with my wife that I have a doubt that I have realized myself because I thought she will make a joke on me.

With little hesitation I conveyed her about the transformation which I noticed in me and the way I perceive reality. As she was also noticing certain changes in me for quite some days, she asked how we would confirm it, because we have never come across someone who has similar experience. So, we thought of searching about people who have shared their experience of enlightenment in internet. But I found people talking about all imaginations other than reality. So, I decided to let live with this experience for sometime without worrying about the reason behind it.

I felt so complete that I didn't even bother to waste time on searching and hearing about others experiences which is not going to make any difference to me. I simply sat on the sofa and observed the objects around; I was totally in the moment. There was no ego (mind) which has dissolved into the existence. In the absolute stillness, there were no thoughts, no fear and no worries. I was totally in the freshness of the eternal now, without any feeling of boredom. I sat there hours together without any slight movement, in fact I felt there is no need to move and miss this moment. It is not possible to explain the happiness in words and the inner peace that I experienced. I felt totally complete without any questions and not interested in doing anything even reading about others experiences. Everything looked meaningless to me except to live in the moment. I was not worried about the future because I was so intensely in the present. Time looked meaningless. In fact I felt there is no time but we practised to live in time. I didn't want to analyse too much about my experience rather I would like to live in it.

Few days has passed like this, I started enjoying being myself. I continued with my usual routine like the way before. Whenever I got time I simply sat and watched the things around. I was feeling so fresh every time as if I was always in a new place. My wife started kidding me that I have got an invisible partner and I am spending so much time with that new partner than with her. I explained her that I was experiencing something new and that feel is not reducing at all even after spending so much time. It is always fresh like it has just started and continuing without any end.

After few days accidently I noticed an Osho book titled Sat-Chit-Anand which I have read half and kept with a page marker, as I have stopped reading for quite sometime. I just opened it and started it from the page where I have left it. He has mentioned clearly that"***Beyond the body and mind, there is a witness which can watch both the body and mind, the material and non material. You cannot go beyond it, you cannot witness it. You have come to the very end of the rope, you have come to the very bottom of the existence. This awareness is called transcendental because it transcends the duality of body-mind. To be centered in it means you have come home***". I closed the book and watched the objects in the room like the way I was doing for few weeks. Whatever the object I looked I was witnessing myself. I confirmed that Truth has happened to me. My inner flower has blossomed and spreading its fragrance. In that moment I cried out of gratitude to existence for showing the Truth and thanked Osho for his guidance.

I have read many of his books and thought that I have understood what he was speaking, but now it has become clear that I didn't understand even a single word, I was just imagining something on my own. To understand him one must experience what he has experienced. If one looks through the mind then one will analyse with all the conditioning and miss the message. All the time he was speaking about Truth but only very few people have understood him. Even I sometimes had a conviction that he was not enlightened because he had criticized all the political and religious leaders around the world. I thought how an enlightened man could speak about others and particularly he made so many sex jokes on religious leaders of that time. But one thing which really surprised me was how a man can be so daring because I have never seen him giving any diplomatic answers. After experiencing the Truth, I understood that only an awakened man has such courage.

Beyond the mind, one fears nothing, when one clearly witnesses that I am not the body and mind but an immortal Self (pure consciousness), there will not be any fear. One who experiences Truth doesn't care about name, fame and what the society thinks. One starts living in the moment without worrying about the future which is bliss.

It has become clear to me that I have transformed myself from mind to no mind, from words to silence, from thinking to living, from suffering to end of suffering. It could happen to anyone irrespective of one's age, gender, race and knowledge. Truth never chooses anyone; it arrives to the one who is ready to receive. I have seen in India, people going to Himalayas to meditate and to attain liberation. This might be partially true because what one basically needs is silence. Our life has been so much conditioned to follow a particular pattern for so many centuries. We were given so many ideas, thoughts, goals and targets to be achieved right from the childhood. All these ideas will take one to the future which is an illusion which exists only in the mind. So we keep living in imaginary future through thinking. This thinking creates so much noise inside and disturbs the inherent peace. If one starts practising silence simply by observing oneself, this noise will slowly calm down over period of time and one's original nature will be revealed to oneself. This is the reason why people might have gone to Himalayas and all the remote locations, just to keep oneself away from the crowd because only in absolute silence man attains his original nature. Naturally the fresh atmosphere and calmness which prevails in Himalayas would stop the mind for few moments and creates stillness. If one can spot this difference and separate the mind from Self (soul), then one can bring awareness and attain liberation. In my opinion place doesn't matter because it happened to me in Germany. It may look strange that people from all around the world travel to India for spiritual experience and to know higher dimension of life but being born and brought up in India, I attained salvation in Germany. What I want to convey is, place is immaterial. In fact whole existence is religious place; one can attain liberation from anywhere.

The experience of the inner Self is also called as awakening because ever since the development of sixth sense (mind), one starts living under the influence of the mind. By identifying oneself with the mind, one lives in a state of deep sleep believing mind's projections as reality. Mind can't survive in the present moment, so it creates so many thoughts by bringing all the past memories and projecting into the future. Anything can happen in the future, there are so many possibilities, so mind creates so many versions of illusions and keep projecting it.

"Mind is a great storyteller. It keeps telling the same story again and again repeatedly to ensure that you remain asleep".

By doing so, it simply takes one away from the present which is life. By believing these illusions as reality, one always lives in the future even though his body remains in the present moment. This is what happening to majority of population around the world. By thinking about the future people miss living in the present. The moment one separates oneself from the mind, all these thoughts will stop. 'Self' which has been suppressed and kept in a dormant state by the mind since childhood will awake. Once it happens, one becomes pure witness of oneself, unaffected by circumstances.

"Once the Self awakens, the mind which was playing lead role will be pushed into the back stage and called once in a while to play support role".

5 Blissfulness

I was totally complete and happy being myself. I realized that nothing needs to be added or achieved to be happy. By taking life seriously I was always in fear. When I started relaxing, it became clear that life is a blessing. I didn't need to push hard for anything. Whatever I do, I have to do it with complete awareness. Once it's done, there is no need to carry the result of the past action and suffer in the present moment. This is what people call as karma. Any action arises out of awareness doesn't carry karma. Being in the present has become my nature and this is the nature of every being. Since people have forgotten their original nature so they suffer.

Most of the times, I simply sat and remained in the state of blissfulness (eternal happiness). It was always fresh, always new every moment. It stayed with me to wherever I go. I experimented that, whether I could have the same experience everywhere, by going to nearby parks, forest, super markets and sometimes while waiting for hair dressing in saloon. It was always the same, irrespective of place. I was roaming like a newborn just watching without any idea of the world. Memory (mind) was there but kept aside and I was using it only when it is really required. I didn't like to read anything particularly about philosophy because I felt that it is not needed anymore as I am already witnessing the Truth. Moreover I didn't want to corrupt the inherent knowledge which is arising in me. I decided to let it be pure, without considering others ideas and concepts.

"Knowledge arises when one starts witnessing the Truth, before that what one considers as knowledge is just an ignorance of the Self"

Actually when one realizes the Self, whatever one has to know, will be revealed to him. He doesn't need any other external source of knowledge. Some of the words like 'Self' has automatically come to me. I wanted to use a word to indicate the layer above the mind and I got the word 'Self', which means our consciousness or life energy. Also I decided to avoid the word 'god' because it projects an image or figure of someone; instead I used the word 'Truth'. By using these words I wrote some quotes, which I thought would help people to come out of their mind and relax in present moment. Because majority of the people are perceiving the world through their head (intellect) and living in imagination without knowing the reality. In fact it can't be even called as living rather as dreaming.

I started sharing some of the quotes on my social media and messaging application. Many people appreciated it by saying that it is very relaxing to read my messages and to take life as it comes. But there was also strong opposition from people who were following traditional religious practices. Some of my relatives advised me, not to read too much and get confused. Also, one of my ex-colleague after seeing the below quote,

"Beyond the senses and mind there is an eternal watcher, who just observes without any judgement just like a newborn. One who arrives here witnesses the Truth in everything and everywhere"

Asked me, from where I was getting all these quotes. I told him that I have been writing it through my experience. He replied how is it possible or legitimate to believe that someone could arrive here without following any cult. I told him that it happened through meditation and it's up to him whether to believe it or not. He replied that it is impossible and not at all authorized by scriptures. It took millions of years of meditation even for Brahma (god of creation as per Hindu mythology) to see the lord. I told him clearly that if one looks through the knowledge (scriptures) then one will miss the reality which is totally different. Again he questioned, whether in your opinion the scriptures are wrong or we shouldn't restrict ourselves to only scriptures. I told him I don't know really, I realized myself and still I need some more time to give a clear explanation for this question.

After few days, again the discussion happened, this time about what god means to me. I replied that God should be an experience and until one carries the knowledge of god, it will drift one away from god. I told him to drop all this knowledge what he has been carrying on his head, then it would not be very difficult to witness the Truth. But he was not convinced and said that I was a kind of intellectual, who has control over one's thoughts. I replied that if it was his assumption then it's perfectly fine. I was neither interested in proving that I have arrived nor bothered about his opinion, which is not going to change the reality. I understood that he has accumulated so much of knowledge about God over the past decade. Suddenly if someone comes and tells that the reality is different, it's general human tendency to reject it.

The scriptures particularly Hindu scriptures are so vast and so many people have interpreted it and translated it. People usually start reading the scriptures to know about god (Truth) but once they get certain clarity, they forget the purpose, why they have started reading the scriptures; rather they become more interested in acquiring more knowledge on god. There is a big difference between knowledge of God and God, because god (infinite) can't be confined into any knowledge which is finite. In India majority of the population are reading the scriptures without understanding this, in the name of following religion. They are under the illusion that they have renounced the materialistic world and made a greater ambition to attain eternal spiritual world after death. It is not their mistake and I don't want to blame them. This dream has been given to them by some senior authority and they are simply following it. But they failed to understand the very simple fact that the moment future comes into picture, it brings the mind. Whatever one thinks about the future, it comes from the mind whatever one dreams about the future, it's the mind. There is no difference between someone who thinks of becoming rich in next 5 years and someone who thinks of entering into eternal world after death. Both are same because both are mind-games. Mind creates an illusion of being spiritual and starts giving different goals and dreams. One can't become spiritual just by reading scriptures and following certain religious practices. The purpose of any religion is to know oneself and to become pure but it is impossible to attain this within the boundary of mind.

"Spirituality is peeling off the thick layer of mind which one has developed over years, in order to reveal one's original nature"

Even after witnessing the Truth I used to pray to God. We have Lord Shiva (god of destruction) photo frame in our home. I had a habit of praying to sun god and Lord Shiva everyday immediately after taking bath. One day a question arose in me, if what I was experiencing is Truth then why we have so many gods and so many sects worshipping different forms of gods in Hinduism. By looking at reality, only Advaita (Vedanta) founded by Adi Sankaracharya, where they follow the oneness (non-duality) appeared realistic, but it is not very wide spread like dualism. In India there are so many sects, reading various scriptures and adventures of gods on earth. Why there exists so many gods when the Truth is one. I asked this question to Cosmic consciousness (Truth) in absolute silence and went to bed. In the middle of the night I woke up and suddenly all the answers has come to me in that moment. I was very much surprised to receive answers which have been hidden for over thousands of years.

Next day morning when my wife woke up, I shared the details of what I have received. After hearing, she also got surprised and told that, what I am talking about is something totally different from the way gods have been traditionally projected and worshipped for thousands of years in Hinduism. We have discussed about it for so many weeks and in the mean time I clearly understood about the facts behind the representation of gods, which has led me to explore the human anatomy, particularly neuroscience because it is impossible for anyone to understand the representation of Hindu gods, without understanding the neuroscience. I was totally shocked to find out that so many minute details have been conveyed through stories. It has become clear that the truth has been hidden in the stories as bits and pieces and it is very difficult for anyone to filter the actual meaning from the vast amount of information which has been orally transmitted and written for over a thousand of years. I wrote down the information about the gods and the meaning behind their representation in a note book. Later we decided to share this information with the world because this information will totally change the world's perception about Hinduism and will lead to new discoveries in history, science and religion. That's the main reason for inking this book, to reveal 2500 years old hidden mysteries of Hinduism.

"Science and theology go hand in hand because both are intellectual approach. For the same reason both enslaves one within the mind"

6 Gods in Hinduism

Let's take a deep insight into the concept of God in Hinduism. Ancient Hindus believed in one god whom they called as Brahman, which means cosmic consciousness or Supreme Being. It is the unchanging unmanifested ultimate reality, but it is the cause of all the changes happening in the world. All the manifested beings are part of this Supreme Being and it is the one which is present inside every being as life force or soul (Nikhilananda, 1947). Only the Self-realized people can experience it, for others it might be difficult to perceive, so they introduced the concept of personal gods. The most important among them is the deity of Nataraja (cosmic dance) {Fig.1} because cosmic consciousness is cause of all the changes happening in this universe and it can't be captured in any single posture other than dancing. It is representation of Brahman itself; I will explain the reason behind it in later section of this chapter {Sec.6.4}. Ancient Hindus started worshipping the cosmic consciousness in the form of Nataraja because the Supreme Being is the cause of all the changes and it can end one's life long sufferings permanently by giving liberation. Another important form they conceptualized during this time is Linga {Fig.2}. I would like to shift the focus on why they worshipped the various forms rather than concerning about the period of their conception. Linga has been misinterpreted in so many ways over the past thousands of years but most of them are incorrect. Basically Linga has three distinguishable structures, the lower base and slightly larger middle portion and a cylindrical sphere protruding from the middle layer. It has been interpreted as the male and female organ which is not true. I will disclose the reason in the later part of this chapter {Sec.6.3}.

Fig.1 Nataraja (Cosmic Consciousness)

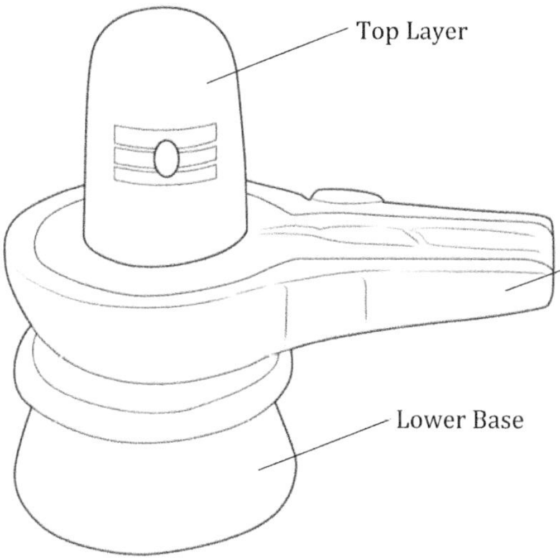

Fig.2 Linga

One more important concept is Trimurti (Trinity)

1.Brahma (God of Creation)

2.Vishnu (God of Protection)

3.Shiva (God of Destruction)

As per the Hindu mythology, Brahma is responsible for creation of the universe and Vishnu is responsible for protection of the universe and Shiva is responsible for destruction of the universe. They live in higher planets and each of them are represented differently, holding different weapons which are meant for killing demons and for various other reasons. So this cycle of creation, protection and destruction keeps continuing again and again and so many universes has been created, protected and destructed so far. There are so many stories for each of these trinity gods particularly more for Vishnu in Hindu scriptures. Whenever there is a problem on earth or when irreligiousness raises Vishnu himself incarnates on earth in various forms and saves earth and re-establish religion. There are so many temples dedicated to Vishnu and Shiva except Brahma. All the major Hindu festivals are celebrated to remember certain important event of these trinity gods in earth.

People who have born in Hindu family might have heard the stories about these trinity gods from their grandparents and parents right from their childhood. There are so many dramas and movies which were made based on these stories. Even I have wondered how the gods are still using the Iron Age weapons which are out dated, when humanity with its limited intelligence has invented and started using very advanced weapons. But the biggest surprise is all of them are not actually weapons as the way they have been described and depicted in the mythology so long. This truth has been hidden intentionally or forgotten in the middle of some centuries. Let's see clearly who these Trinity gods and what their weapons actually represents and why there are called as creator, protector and destroyer.

6.1 Brahma (God of Creation)

Brahma {Fig.3} is called as the God of creation and his one and only duty is to create the universe. He is represented as an old man with long beard, four heads looking in all four directions with a single body, shown as sitting in lotus posture on lotus flower. He is slightly decorated with ornaments and has four hands holding Vedas (scriptures) and lotus in upper hands, beads and water mug (Kamandala) in lower hands. There are different versions of stories about Brahma's birth, some say that Brahma originated from Shiva and some claim that he sprang from

Vishnu's navel and some other version claims that the unmanifested Supreme Being (Brahman) has manifested himself as Brahma. But as we move further, we can understand from where he has actually come from.

Fig.3 Brahma (God of Creation)

Let us explore what has been actually conveyed through the graphical representation of Brahma. If we observe {Fig.3}, the four heads of the Brahma are actually meant to indicate the four senses in the head, 1. Eyes (vision), 2. Nose (smell), 3. Mouth (taste) and 4. Ears (hearing) and the single body to represent the fifth sense 5. Body (touch).

Usually every child {Fig.4} arrives in the world as a pure consciousness with partially developed five senses without the sixth sense (mind) which needs more time to develop after birth. So the human body has been depicted as Brahma in Trimurti. He holds beads in his lower right hand which denotes the time, because the body can live only for limited period of time as it changes over time and vanishes back into the existence. This is also the reason why Brahma has been depicted as an old man with beard. He holds lotus in his upper right hand and Vedas in his upper left hand. It is believed that Vedas have originated from Brahma which we will see how and also the meaning of the lotus. He holds a water mug (Kamandala) in his lower left hand to show that he creates the illusionary materialistic world.

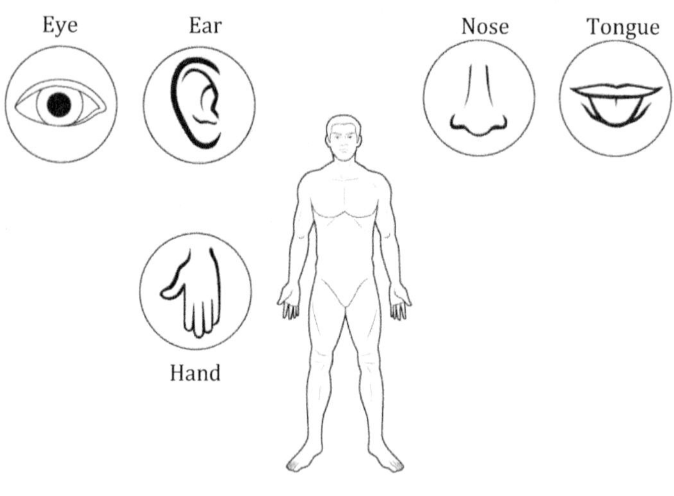

Fig.4 Five Senses of Human Being

Also there is a story that Brahma has created Saraswathi and fallen in love with her for her beauty and later made her as his consort. This story is made to create awareness that if one identifies too much with body and heeds to bodily desires then one can go to any extent to even marry one's own daughter. These kinds of barbaric incidents are still happening in the world. So this is one of the reasons why Brahma is not worshipped widely as other two gods. But the actual reason is Brahma (body) can't be creative without the sixth sense (mind). That's why there are very few temples for Brahma located in northern India.

Then how Brahma develops his sixth sense? To understand it, we need to look at Brahma's consort Saraswathi {Fig.5}. She is represented as holding a musical instrument called Veena and other two hands holding beads and Vedas like Brahma. She is called as the Goddess of Knowledge.

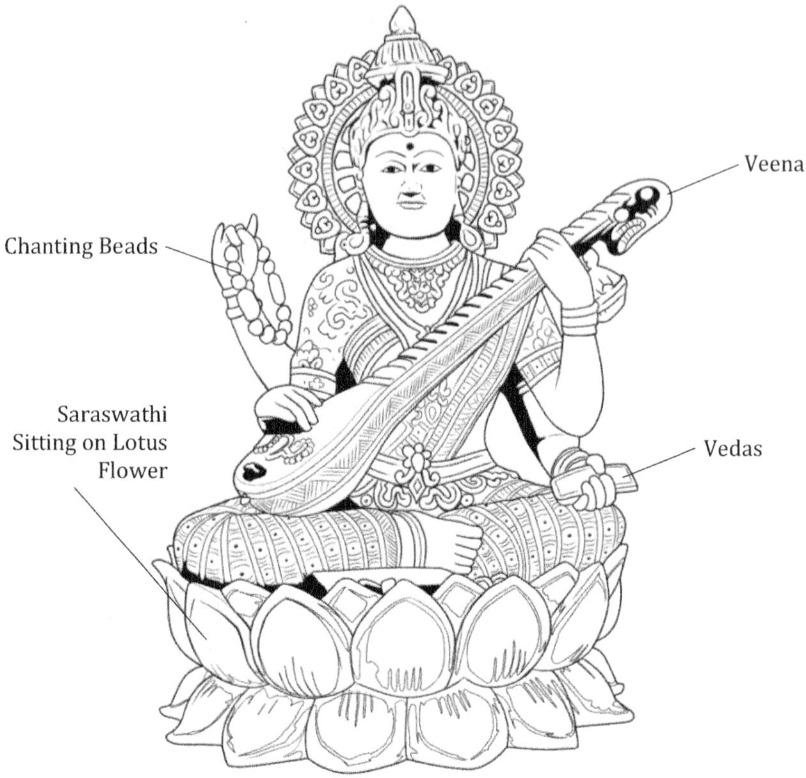

Fig.5 Saraswathi (Goddess of Knowledge)

In India people celebrate Saraswathi pooja to acknowledge the birth of Knowledge and it is usually considered as an auspicious day for children to start their education. Even today parents enroll their kids in kindergarten during this day, so that the child will excel in education with the blessings of goddess of Knowledge. If we analyse closely there arises a question why she is called as the Goddess of Knowledge and what is the relation between knowledge and musical instrument. No one knows the answer and some people will tell some illogical stories which are not true. To know the answer we need to analyse how a child develops knowledge. As mentioned earlier child arrives as a pure consciousness, it witnesses everything around just like an observer without any idea. Then someone (usually mother) introduces the name of the child which is basically a sound which enters through the ear. If we look at what the child is hearing as a sound, is basically a language. After repetitive hearing of its name, it starts identifying with its name. In the mean time the child also hears about objects and people around by their names and starts identifying everything by the name. In its first 5 to 6 years, child has to hear the sounds of any particular language in order to speak properly, when it hears the sounds through the ears it gets registered as a memory in the brain, only then it builds up as a language. This language forms the foundation for understanding about the world around which we call as Knowledge. So knowledge develops not just by seeing the objects around but by hearing about the objects. Basically knowledge means naming the objects and events by articulating different sounds.

As the language gives the child a unique identity by a name and by giving so it introduces the concept of duality which means, identifying oneself as subject "I" and everything else as an object. So language is the knowledge and it develops by hearing the sound through the ears. Even the scripts of the language are just symbols assigned to a sound. There are so many languages which doesn't have any scripts at all. Sanskrit which was very predominantly used in ancient times particularly for religious practices doesn't have any scriptures for long time. So it has been orally transferred from one to another as a sound.

Thomas J. Hopkins who worked as professor of Religious studies in Franklin and Marshall college said that "***Sanskrit words are not just arbitrary labels assigned to phenomena; they are the sound forms of objects, actions***

and attributes related to the corresponding reality in the same way as visual forms and different only in being perceived by the ear and not by eye".

So knowledge is a sound. That's why goddess Saraswathi has been represented with a musical instrument and called as Goddess of Knowledge. So this is how knowledge develops in a child. It has to hear from someone as a sound and is registered in its brain as a memory and develops into a language. In fact child starts listening to the sounds of the external environment even before birth when it is still in the mother's womb. So basically sound is considered as a source of knowledge in Hindu mythology.

To know exactly how the sixth sense develops by hearing the sound, we need to look more closely at anatomy of human ear {Fig.6}, which is very important before moving further to the next god in Trimurti. Human ear is basically divided into three regions, outer, middle and inner ear. Part of the outer ear called as pinna is the one which is normally visible and it just acts like an antenna to receive the sound waves and passes it into auditory canal. Then the sound travels through the auditory canal (a very narrow region). Here the sound gets amplified and enters into the middle ear region and it hits the ear drum which is called as tympanic membrane. Tympanic membrane vibrates and passes the sound into another three small bone structures called Malleus, Incus and Stapes and transmits the sound to the oval window. This oval window passes sound into inner ear which has three main parts called semicircular canals, vestibule and cochlea. Semicircular canals and vestibule are filled with two different types of fluids called perilymph and endolymph and there are finer hair cells within this fluid which are responsible for maintaining the equilibrium of the head. Lower part of the vestibule connects to the cochlea. Cochlea is a very sensitive part of the ear and it is also called as the organ of hearing. It's name has been derived from the Greek Word 'kokhliās' which means snail because it looks like a snail shell, this is the region where the sound gets converted into electrical impulses and from there signals reaches the auditory cortex of the brain.

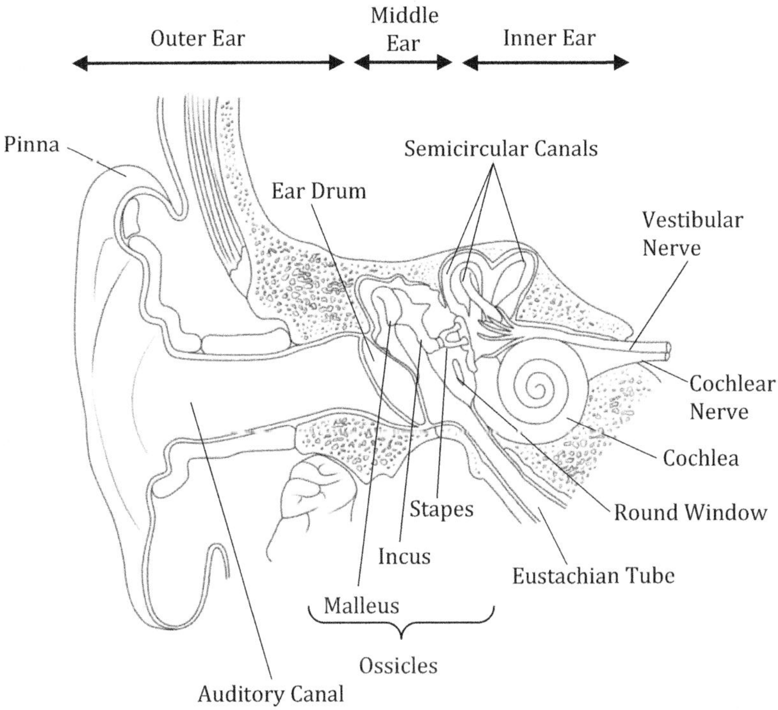

Fig.6 Anatomy of Human Ear

It is also important to observe the cross section of cochlea {Fig.7} it has three sections; upper and lower sections are called as scala vestibula and scala tympanic which are filled with sodium rich fluid called perilymph. Middle section is cochlear duct which is filled with potassium rich fluid called endolymph; also it encloses the auditory organ called organ of Corti. The organ of Corti has finer hair cells whose tip is bathed in endolymph fluid which are responsible for hearing. Again these hair cells are of two types, outer hair cells and inner hair cells (Pujol, Nouvian, & Lenoir, 2016).

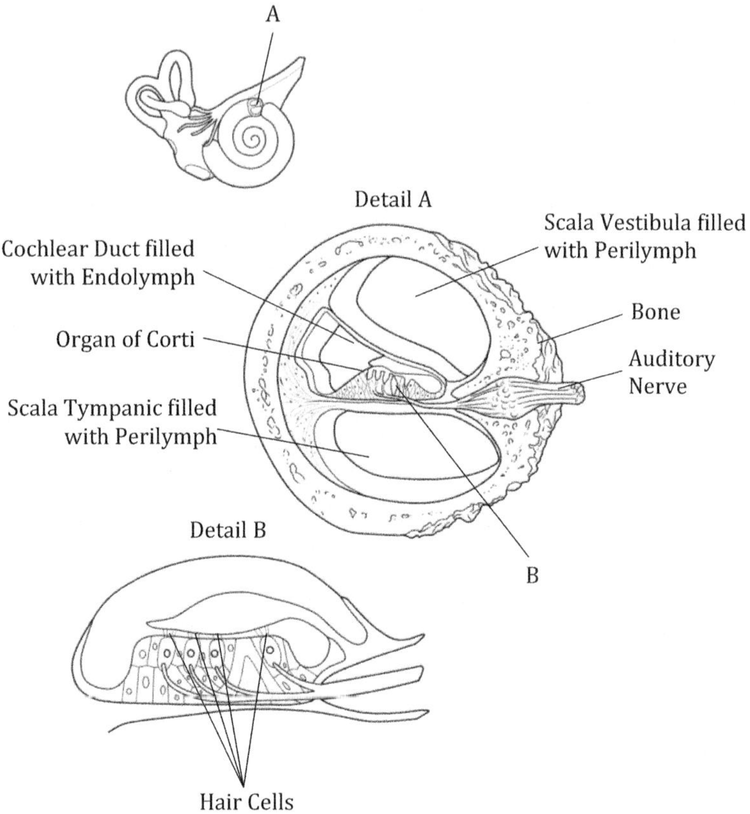

Fig.7 Cross Section of Cochlea

These hair cells are arranged in such a way to receive sounds of various frequencies. If the cochlea is uncoiled, the beginning of the cochlea is called base and the end of the cochlea is called apex. In the base it receives sounds of high frequency and in the apex it receives the sounds with low frequency. When the sound passes inside the cochlea, due to the potential difference between the fluids inside the cochlear chambers, the corresponding hair cells gets triggered which generates the signal and send it to the brain. So this is how sounds of different frequencies are converted into corresponding electrical impulses inside the cochlea (Hayes, Ding, Salvi, & Allman, 2013) (Gale Sloan Thompson, 2015). So, once the sound enters the ear, it travels as sound wave (acoustic) till the ear drum and then it becomes a mechanical vibration in the middle ear region and reaches the oval window and finally becomes an electrochemical signal in the cochlea and reaches the brain.

Suddenly it may appear like a spiritual book has turned into a science book and describing about anatomy of ear and process of hearing. But that's what Hinduism is all about. It describes how the man develops in each stage with perfect understanding of science. So knowledge is the sound, it enters through ears and reaches the brain. With this clarity we move to the next god in the Trimurti.

6.2 Vishnu (God of Protection)

In Hinduism, Vishnu {Fig.8} is usually represented in a sleeping posture on Adisesha a serpent. According to Vedic literature, Adisesha is a thousand headed snake floating in an ocean of milk called Vaikunta (higher planet) and it acts like Vishnu's bed. It is said to be part of Vishnu and it also incarnates along with Vishnu whenever he incarnates to re-establish the religion.

If one observes carefully the ear anatomy as showed in the {Fig.6} beginning from the outer ear to middle ear, one can easily relate to Vishnu's sleeping posture on Snake {Fig.8}. Even though Snakes doesn't have any visible ears they are well known for their hearing capabilities because its whole body acts like an ear in receiving vibration from the earth. So symbolically snake has been shown to indicate the ears. The hood of this serpent {Fig.8} is nothing but the outer covering of the ear and Vishnu's whole body represents the passage of the auditory canal up to (tympanic membrane) ear drum. In some representations one can find his consort (Lakshmi) sitting at his feet and massaging his legs. She basically represents the ear drum.

Vishnu holds two weapons chakra (Disc) in his right hand and conchshell in his left hand {Fig.10}, which are given to represent the cochlea of right and left ear. There is a clever reason behind the distinctive representation of the cochleas of the right and left ear. So much research has been conducted on this topic in the last century and the modern science has discovered that both ears behave differently and receives different kinds of sounds. The right ear has a distinctive advantage when it comes to processing speech and language related functions and left ear is good for processing tonal stimuli and music (Sininger & Cone-Wesson, 2004). This difference is mainly attributed to the left and right hemispheres of the brain which process the auditory signals coming from the right and left ear which we will discuss in detail in later sections.

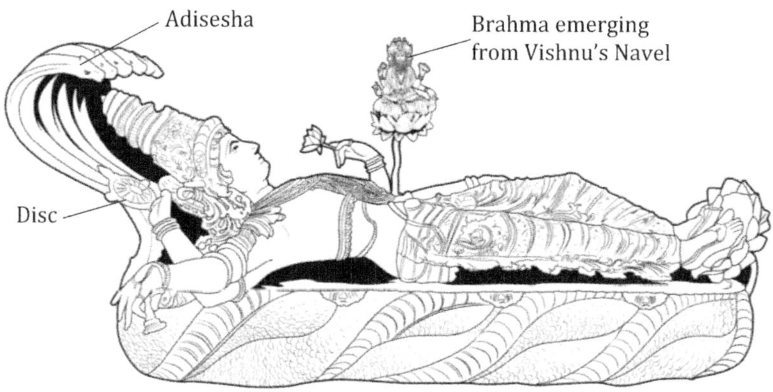

Fig.8 Vishnu in Sleeping Posture

As we have seen in {Fig.6}cochlea is coiled in horizontal axis with respect to the outer ear, this cochlea is taken out from both the ears and kept as weapons next to Vishnu's ears in horizontal axis. The Disc is kept to show the sharpness of the right ear in processing rapidly changing signals and conchshell at left ear to show its speciality in processing music. So these two weapons are the representations of cochlea in two ears and their importance in receiving sound and converting them into electrical impulses and sending it to the brain through vestibulocochlear nerve.

Brahma is represented as seated on Lotus flower which has emerged from Vishnu's navel in {Fig.8}. Some people have misinterpreted this as showing the connection between mother and a child in the womb. Ancient Hindus are not less intelligent to represent this well known fact. But they have revealed something more valuable which mankind has been trying to figure out, 'How the mind develops in a child'? We have already seen that in a child, sixth sense (mind) develops by hearing the sounds through the ear and getting registered it as a memory in the brain. If we look at the half hemisphere of the brain {Fig.9}, it looks exactly like the lotus in which Brahma is sitting. They have represented lotus as brain. So the connection between ear and brain is represented as a connection between Vishnu and Brahma's lotus. They played a great trick by representing Brahma (body seated on Lotus) very small compared to size of Vishnu (ear) that's how this truth has been hidden for so many thousands of years. Now we know from science that our right ear is connected to the left brain and left ear is connected to the right brain.

From the representation of Vishnu and his weapons along with his connection to Brahma, it is very clear that ancient Hindus were highly advanced in science. They have cross sectioned and studied the complete human body and its anatomy very minutely for thousands of years, well before the invention of high resolution microscopes and scanning equipments. Because some of the structures are in the size of microns which are not at all possible to look through naked eyes without any equipment. It is really surprising that how they have analyzed each and every detail, this shows that they were far ahead from rest of the world when it comes to science.

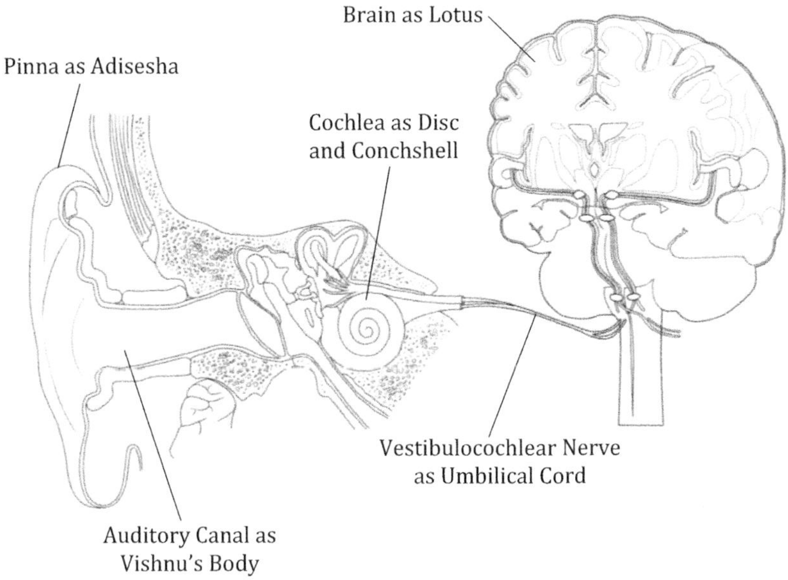

Fig.9 Auditory Pathways

I would like to show and explain more clearly from another representation of Vishnu {Fig.10}. Here he is represented in standing posture and he has two upper and lower hands. One can observe the extraordinary size of the ear, disproportionate to other facial features to show that he is sound which enters through ears. Right upper hand holding 'Disc', which represents the cochlea of the right ear, positioned exactly next to right ear and left upper hand holding the 'conchshell' which represents the cochlea of the left ear positioned exactly next to left ear.

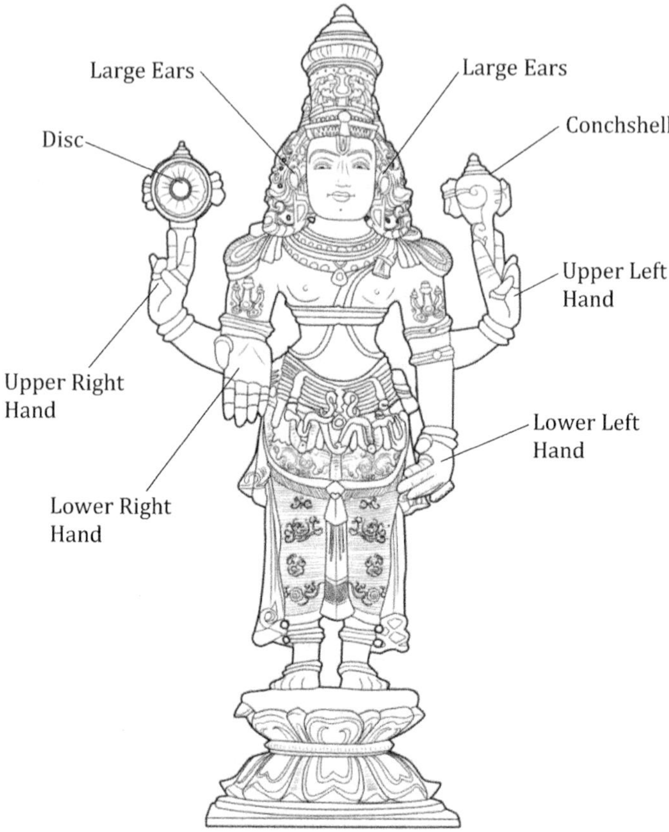

Fig.10 Vishnu in Standing Posture

Among all the senses, ears are the one which has capability to concentrate intensely. Those who are good at listening are the ones who have very good memory. Disc of the right ear symbolically represents the sharpness, concentration and focus. As mentioned before right ear has an advantage in processing language related functions which is connected to the left hemisphere of the brain, because of this reason left hemisphere of the brain has been considered as a language dominant area of the brain (Ocklenburg & Gunturkun, 2018). Basically right ear is very sensitive and sharper than the left ear, that's why lower right hand is positioned above the lower left hand to show the sensitivity and dominance of right ear over the left ear.

This advancement in understanding the evolution of man has made them to cleverly represent how the sixth sense develops. Once the knowledge (sound) enters through ears, mind develops. Also as per the mythology, Brahma tried to reach Vishnu by travelling through the stem of the lotus but he couldn't reach him even after travelling for thousands of years, so he came back. Later he started meditating for millions of years, in spite of his effort he didn't see Vishnu directly but he visualised him in his head (mind) and started creating the Universe as per his instructions.

It is very clear that no one can locate the mind. Everyone knows that the mind is hidden within the body, but unlike other organs, it doesn't have any shape. Even if one makes an effort to spot the mind, all his effort leads to failure because the effort itself will be made by the mind. So finally one has to accept mind as god and start listening to its orders. This is the actual meaning of the story. So once the mind develops, it starts controlling the body (five senses). Even though mind doesn't have any shape, they have given a shape to the mind through Vishnu.

When the mind develops man becomes creative and starts creating things through his intellect. As mind can imagine and generate thoughts and ideas but it can't make it into reality on its own. So it uses the body, the other five senses, just like a commander commanding his soldiers. So all the other senses obey the order of the mind and starts creating the world, means materialistic objects around. This is the reason why Brahma has been called as creator because creation happens through Brahma (body) but he can't create it by himself. He creates by receiving instructions from the mind which is Vishnu. Every human being is Brahma and Vishnu together. Through our intellect we have created everything out of nothing. This creation is happening for so many thousands of years and we keep inventing new objects to the already existing ones and it keeps increasing. But whatever we have created, this materialistic world has come from the Vishnu (mind) and it has been made into a reality by the Brahma (body).

As soon as the mind develops man starts knowing about the things around, when he starts learning he becomes knowledgeable. Naturally through his knowledge he starts acquiring wealth.

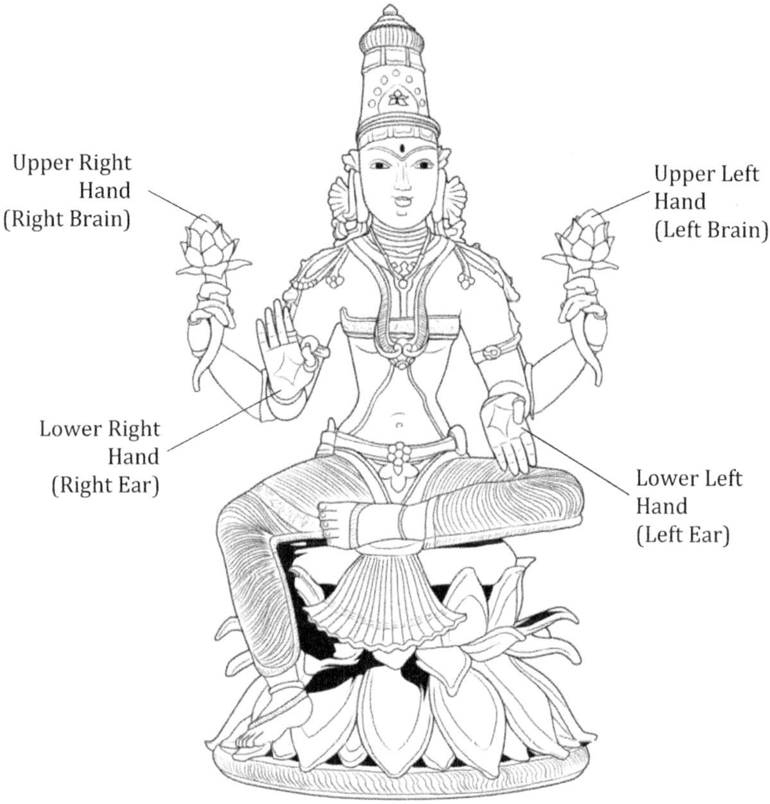

Fig.11 Lakshmi

This is the reason why the Hindus have represented Lakshmi {Fig.11} as Vishnu's consort. Also, it is said that she has taken various incarnations along with Vishnu. She is considered as Goddess of wealth, fortune and prosperity. There is a common saying in India, by worshipping Vishnu; one will also get the blessings of Lakshmi because wealth (Lakshmi) is the by-product of knowledge (Vishnu). She is also represented with four hands, two upper hands holding lotus and two empty lower hands. The two upper hands holding lotus represents the two hemisphere of the brain. Lower right hand denotes the right ear which is connected to left hemisphere of the brain and the lower left hand denotes the left ear which is connected to the right hemisphere of the brain. Lower right hand positioned above the lower left hand to denote the sensitivity of right ear over the left ear same as discussed in {Fig.10} This is the actual meaning of the statue.

In India, people consider money as Lakshmi and when someone acquires wealth it is believed that it is only because of Lakshmi's blessings. We can find her idol or photo at all the cash counters right from small shops to multi storey super markets. When knowledge (sound) enters through the ears and registers as a memory in the brain, it develops as a mind and becomes intelligence. To survive in this materialistic world one needs wealth but wealth is a by product of one's intelligence. So naturally wealth follows the intelligence.

It is not always necessary that highly educated people has high level of intelligence. But highly intelligent people are the ones who have higher capability to create more wealth. There were so many uneducated people who have made fortunes from nothing because of their intelligence. Vishnu is called as Protector God because to protect this earned wealth or to safe guard existing wealth, one needs the intelligence (mind). For the same reason Vishnu is being decorated with more gold ornaments and jewellery. He is one of the wealthiest Hindu gods and his temples generate highest revenue annually through donations and public offerings in India.

The whole materialistic world that we have created is because of his potency, means because of mind's capability. All inventions right from wheel, steam engine, electricity, automobile to space ship everything was once conceived as an idea and made into reality by Brahma (body) through guidance from Vishnu (mind).

Another important thing is, it is said that scriptures are originated from Brahma through the instructions from Vishnu. Brahma is considered as the original authority of the Vedic literature known as Vedas, which literally means knowledge. As mind (Vishnu) can only imagine, but cannot create anything so it has instructed the body (Brahma) to write it. This is how Vedas has been born, but in Indian mythology it is described as, Brahma sitting in Brahmaloka (Brahma's planet) heard it from Vishnu who resides in Vishnuloka (Vishnu's planet). While representing as a statue they have positioned Brahma above Vishnu but in the stories they have maintained the order properly, by describing that Brahma lives in a planet called Brahmaloka which will annihilate after certain millions of years but Vishnu lives in an even higher spiritual planet called Vishnuloka which is eternal. This was told to convey that mind is above the body and body will annihilate, but mind which is knowledge will be transferred from one to another and lives as far as the mankind exists. For the same reason Brahma has been represented as an old man to show that body becomes old and Vishnu (mind/knowledge) always remains young and never gets old.

In most of the Vishnu's statues his forehead is covered with a symbol which starts from the forehead and covers almost half of the eyes. This symbol is called as 'Namam'. Let's see {Fig.12} and understand what does this symbol actually represents.

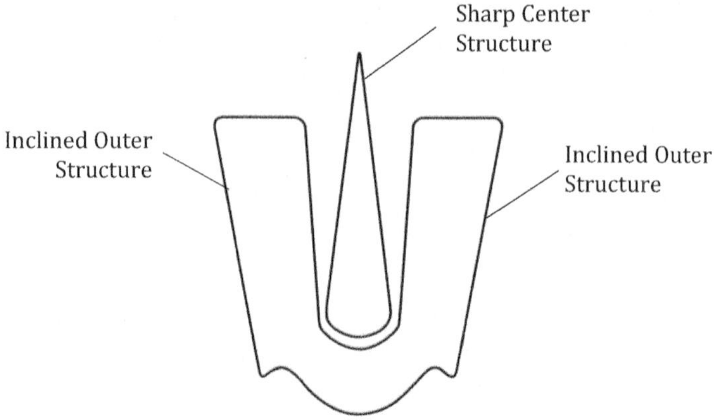

Fig.12 Vishnu's Namam Symbol

It has three structures, two outer inclined structures usually represented in white colour and a sharp center structure which is represented in red colour. The center structure is broader at the base and sharper at the top; also it is longer than the other two outer structures. This Namam symbol is meant to show the connection between both the ears and the brain. It can be very clearly understood from the human auditory system diagram {Fig.13} that the right and left ears are slightly inclined in its vertical axis exactly like the outer structures of Namam symbol and the brain which is broader at the base and converges sharply at the top represents the middle structure. This is the actual meaning of Namam, where knowledge (mind) is represented as a symbol.

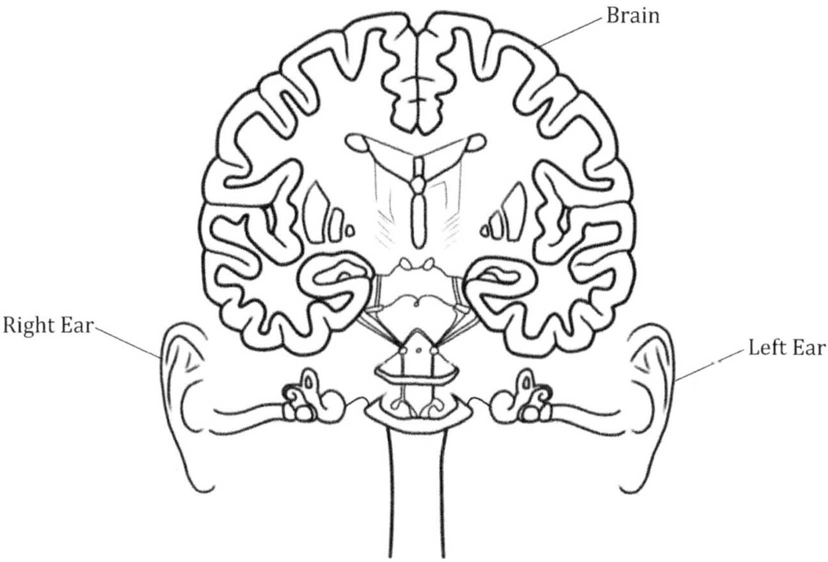

Fig.13 Human Auditory System

Usually this symbol covers half of Vishnu's eyes which denotes, that when one carries knowledge in his head, he will not be able to look at the reality because knowledge is an illusion which separates one from the reality. This happens to everyone, when one looks through the mind, one starts living in an imagination within the boundaries of the mind and observed in its projection which is not real.

"Looking through the mind is like blindfolding oneself and identifying the external environment in accordance with ideas and projections given by it".

So Vishnu is the sixth sense which is the creative potential of mankind but it separates one from Truth, from God and so from reality. The moment sixth sense develops child loses its connection with consciousness (Self or soul) and becomes slave of the mind.

Fig.14 Garuda Vishnu's Vehicle

If one looks at Vishnu's vehicle, he uses Garuda shown in {Fig.14} which is actually an Eagle. As we have seen in the earlier description that sound is the knowledge and Vishnu is the God of Knowledge. So how the sound travels, it travels in the medium of air in the form of wave. So eagle which is considered as king of birds is represented as his vehicle. This is how ancient Hindus have represented the knowledge and its development as mind by characterising it as god through various stories and images.

Even though sound, knowledge and mind look different, they all are forms of Vishnu. Sound is a wave which contains information about certain object or idea. When someone utters a word, it is a sound which is Vishnu. When this sound enters through ears it becomes the knowledge which is also Vishnu and when all this knowledge accumulates and develops as a mind, this is also Vishnu. Most of the languages are originated as sound and later got its scripts over the period of its evolution. If we listen to a language which is unknown to us then it is just a kind of sound. But if we know the language then we are able to understand the information of the sound by correlating the received sound with the already stored memory in the brain, because we have already made the base by learning that particular language.

In olden days, most of the secrets were transferred as a sound through the ears. There are many primitive languages which still exist today without any scripts. Actually Vedas (Hindu scriptures) which are originated from Sanskrit were mostly transferred as sound through ears and memorized for thousands of years. Its time period has been calculated only after it has been written. So every child's mind develops by hearing the sounds (information) about an objects and events, even before getting introduced to written format.

Vishnu has mainly 108 temples which are called as Divya Desams (holy places). As per religious beliefs, if one visits all these 108 temples within his life time then he will never take birth again, means attains liberation. But actually all the 108 temples are not in the earth, only 106 are located in the earth and the remaining 2 places were said to be in higher planets which are not possible for anyone to enter with materialistic body. It is true because knowledge which enters through both the ears as a sound, registers as a memory in the brain and becomes mind. No one can be able to locate the mind. Unless one separates oneself from the mind through meditation, one can't differentiate Vishnu (mind) which is within the Brahma (body). So the last two temples are not outside but within everyone. When one goes beyond the mind, one crosses both these temples and becomes one with Supreme Being (Brahman).

An uniqueness is followed in the construction of most of these 108 Vishnu temples. In all the temples, Vishnu (main deity) is represented in different forms and is located straight to the temple's main entrance. But just in front of the deity there will be a wall where his vehicle Garuda (eagle) is positioned and covers the view of main deity. In order to see the deity one must cross Garuda. This is also meant to show that mind hides inside you and it's very difficult to find it.

So our ancestors have conceptualised the body as Brahma (God of creation) with four heads (four senses) and a body (fifth sense). Mind (sixth sense) as Vishnu (God of preservation) by showing the connection between ears and brain. No other civilization in the world has such an intelligence to represent graphically, body as Brahma and mind as Vishnu before thousands of years. So definitely they were far advanced in science and whatever they have created as forms and told as stories, were all made to indicate body and mind and science behind its evolution.

6.3 Shiva (God of Destruction)

Shiva is called as destroyer for some reasons which I will explain later. We have seen how a man evolves from body and then into second layer mind. But evolution of the man wouldn't stop there. To become complete, man has to realize his Self (soul or consciousness). I will be using mostly 'Self' to indicate the third layer of the man throughout this book. So to represent the completeness of man, they have made Linga.

As I have briefly described about Linga in the beginning of this chapter. It is basically made of three structures, the lower base and the slightly larger middle portion and cylindrical sphere at the top. Let's see what does Linga {Fig.15} actually represents.

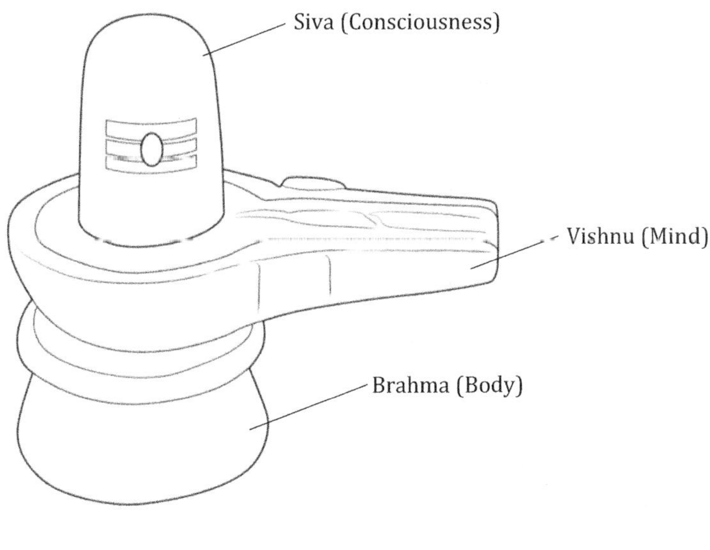

Fig.15 Linga

The lower substrate represents Brahma (body) which includes all the five senses. The middle layer is Vishnu (mind). We can clearly see that the middle layer is just the representation of ear passage which we have seen in anatomy of the ear {

Fig.6} and in the sleeping posture of Vishnu {Fig.8}. Also we have seen how the sixth sense (mind) develops. Knowledge enters as a sound through ears and becomes mind, so the middle layer is Vishnu. The top cylindrical sphere represents Shiva to show the infiniteness, completeness and wholeness. It shows the oneness. When a man attains his complete potential, he becomes infinite. He will not identify anymore with his body and mind, he becomes one with existence. So whoever has attained liberation has become Linga himself. But it would have become difficult for people to worship Linga with so many misinterpretations. So our ancestors have made a more detailed representation of how a man become, when he attains his original nature and they called him as Shiva. Whoever attains liberation becomes Shiva.

Let's take a look at {Fig.16} which shows Shiva sitting in lotus posture, represented with four hands like other two gods which we have seen earlier. He holds a weapon called as Trisool (Trident) in the upper right hand and a musical instrument called Damaru in the upper left hand and his two lower hands are kept at the bottom of abdomen to show his meditative nature.

When man meditates and attains liberation, he becomes a yogi and becomes one with existence. He goes beyond the body and mind (Brahma and Vishnu). He starts looking at reality rather than through the mind. His inner world which mind has created with so many desires and goals to be fulfilled in future will be destroyed by the consciousness. This is the reason why Shiva has been called as destroyer. He doesn't destroy any universe or planets as the way people have imagined for thousands of years. He destroys the illusionary world created by the mind. Consciousness removes the illusions and brings the bliss (eternal happiness) which man has been longing throughout his life. Shiva is almost represented in bare body to show how a man becomes unattached to worldly things after enlightenment.

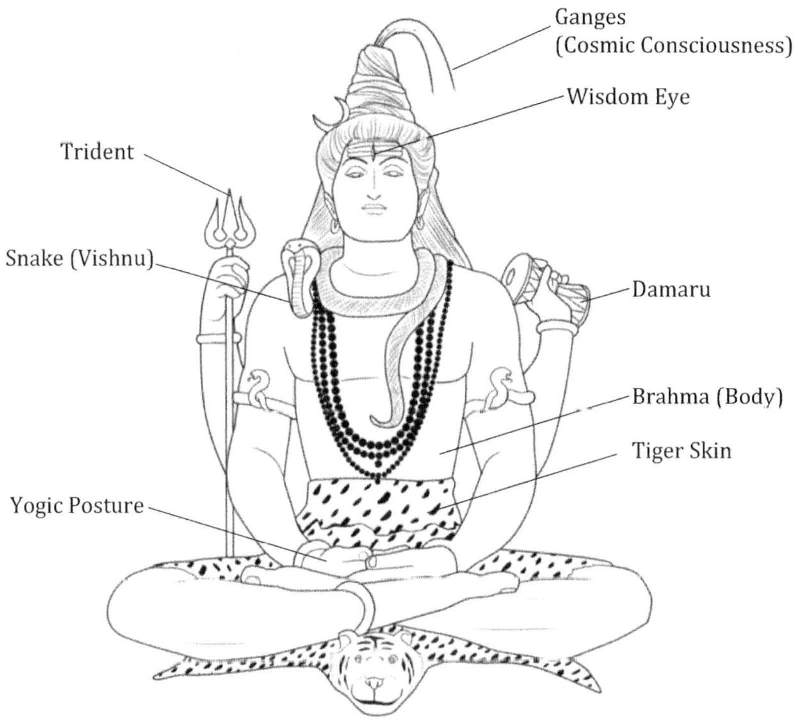

Fig.16 Shiva

His body represents Brahma and snake on the neck represents Vishnu who rests in the ocean of milk on the snake, which is mind. Knowledge enters as sound through ears because snake is known for its hearing capabilities, so it has been shown as mind.

Shiva's face has been depicted in the state of calmness, to show the arrival of inner peace.

Basically they have tried to show Linga as a man, by showing the three layers in the same order as body, mind and consciousness. His third eye known as wisdom eye is shown opened to symbolically represent the awakening, where as in Vishnu's forehead it is covered by knowledge (Namam). This knowledge (Namam) has been taken out and shown as Trident (weapon) in Shiva's right hand with the same three structures connected by a straight rod at the bottom. The two outer curved structures represent the ears and middle structure which is broader at the base and sharper at the top represents the brain and the extended rod represents the complete spinal cord. The only difference between the Namam and Trident is the extended rod at the bottom, which is made shorter in Namam to make it appear totally different but both Namam and trident represents knowledge. Here they have shown mind as a weapon in the form of Trident by representing the ears along with complete central nervous system as shown in {Fig.17}. One who becomes Shiva uses his knowledge as weapon (Trident) rather than identifying with it. Shiva wouldn't identify himself with his mind, intellect anymore. Shiva can clearly separate his mind from his Self. Knowing oneself is the actual wisdom. He has mind but will be used only when it is required. He wouldn't live under the control of the sixth sense (mind), which I will explain in detail with another story in later section.

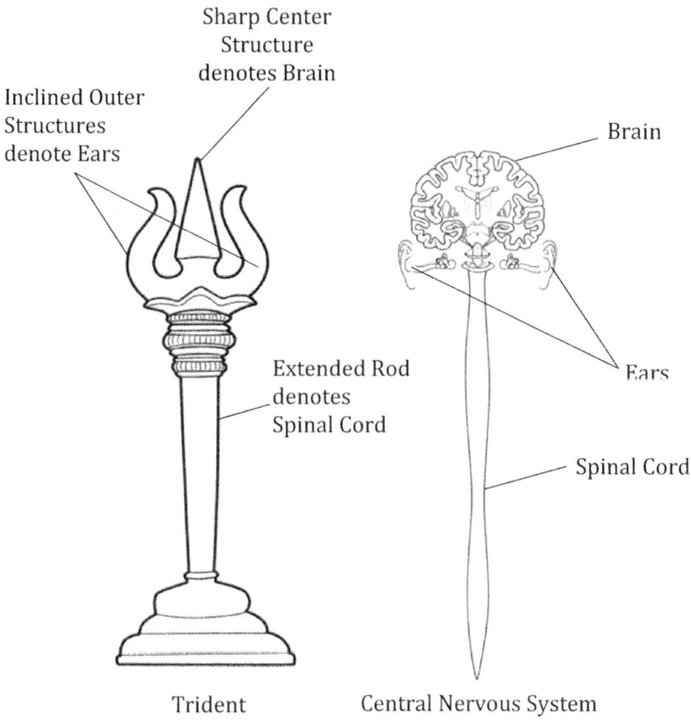

Fig.17 Trident and Central Nervous System

Shiva has freed himself from the mind, which is actually liberation. His forehead has symbol with three horizontal lines to show the order of body, mind and consciousness along with the third eye, shown in {Fig.18}. This is the actual order of the completely evolved man who has attained his highest potential, who has transcended his nature from limited to unlimited.

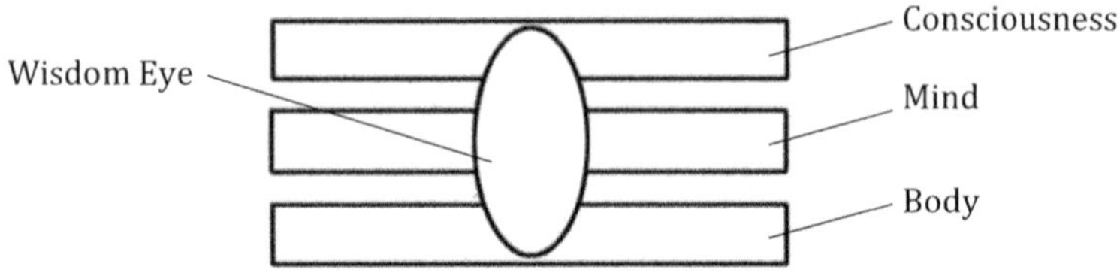

Fig.18 Symbol on Shiva's Forehead

Next if we look at Shiva's head {Fig.16}, there is a half moon on right side and Ganges (Perennial River which originates from Himalayas) flowing from left side. The half moon on the right side indicates the coolness because Shiva remains always cool without worrying about the future.

In Hinduism there is a belief that if one takes bath in Ganges, all the sins committed in his life will be washed away. So almost every authentic Hindu goes to Ganges, at least once in lifetime particularly in their old age, to take a holy bath and wash-off all the sins committed throughout the life. But the actual message is one has to take bath in cosmic consciousness (Brahman) which they have represented as Ganges. Basically Sin is a feeling of guiltiness about the past actions and it will not disappear by taking bath in a river. Only cosmic consciousness can take anyone completely away from the past and makes him to live in present moment. So cosmic consciousness (Brahman) has been indirectly represented as Ganges and the message has been conveyed to take bath in Brahman to wash away the past actions.

Shiva is the representation of the Linga and the Ganges flowing from Shiva's head is to indicate the infiniteness. Cosmic consciousness is the cause of all changes, so it has been shown like water. As consciousness doesn't have any form but it expresses itself in various forms like a tree, fish, insect, bird, animal and human being etc. Similarly water doesn't have any form but it will take the form of the vessel holding it. So basically by depicting Ganges on Shiva's head our ancestors has shown the infiniteness of the Self-realized man. There is also a reason why it has been shown on the left side of the head. When a man attains liberation, he starts hearing the sound of Brahman (Supreme Being) on the left side of the head. It is not an audible sound in the form of frequency to be heard through ears which I have already described about my experience in Chapter {4}. So when consciousness arrives, it arrives with a sound and to show the sound, they have given the Damaru, a kind of musical instrument in the left hand. This instrument can't produce any rhythmic sound like any other musical instruments but it can make only certain type of sound which can't be understood. That's how the sound of cosmic consciousness is; it can't be understood because it is the sound of the source which is beyond the intellectual mind to understand.

Mostly Shiva is represented as sitting on the tiger skin to show that he has overcome all his desires and attained Samadhi (oneness). He is shown as wearing some beads but not with any jewels like the way Vishnu is decorated. Because when one knows the truth, when one knows the reality that all this gold and diamond ornaments are manmade illusions which can't bring eternal inner happiness, one will not be interested in decorating oneself with meaningless jewellery anymore. When one identifies that he is not body and mind, he finds happiness within himself and becomes contented with what he has and starts living the life of renounced. He may be surrounded by any kind of luxury but the luxury will not make any sense to him. He wouldn't hanker for temporary, illusionary happiness because he always remains in an eternal blissfulness.

Shiva is also been portrayed as Guardian of cemetery (Aghori). Cemetery is a place of great significance because irrespective of whatever wealth, knowledge and fame one has accumulated over the years, he has to leave everything and has to depart as the way one has arrived. It directly conveys the brutal truth that nothing is permanent in this life and also the concept of rich and poor doesn't exist. If one understands this reality then one will not waste his life in chasing illusionary materialistic things. Shiva is called as Guardian of cemetery because Cemetery denotes death but here it doesn't mean actual death but death of the mind, removal of illusion. Until there is a mind, the materialistic world which we have created looks real. When one comes out of the mind, he understands the reality. Death is again a concept given by the society and it has strongly rooted into our mind since thousands of years. As we live our whole life identifying ourselves with the body and mind, we create so many relationships, wealth and attach ourselves so much to what we have created. Because of this attachment to the wealth and people (relations), death which separates us away from body and mind looks like reality. When one meditates and transforms one's identity into the inner Self, one realises he is pure consciousness which doesn't have any memory and also mortality. One clearly understands that the consciousness of the Supreme Being has taken the shape of the body and will disappear into the same Supreme Being after sometime; it has neither birth nor death. Shiva is a pure conscious being; he knows that death is an illusion just like all other illusions. Whoever attains salvation becomes Shiva, irrespective of gender.

Linga is also called as Swayambhu which means manifested on its own or without any origin. Hinduism has clearly indicated that no one can help someone to become Shiva, one has to attain his liberation oneself. Becoming Shiva is like a rebirth because throughout the life one has lived like a Brahma (body) under the control of Vishnu (mind). One can experience the actual freedom only after disconnecting oneself from the mind which ends the decades of mental slavery. That's what it exactly means, one has to meditate and attain the Shivahood, which is the representation of completely evolved man. Ancient Hindus have tried their best to show how a man attains liberation and what his qualities are. Like other religions, Hinduism also has only three layers body, mind and consciousness (Self).

Shiva also has so many temples in India and in all the temples he is worshipped in the form of Linga but not as a Statue. In most of the temples we can find Nataraja (cosmic dance) on the left side of Linga, but this Nataraja has great significance and it represents the Supreme Being (Brahman) itself which I explain later {Sec.6.4}. The inner sanctum (Garbhagriha) where the Linga is stationed will be positioned exactly straight from the temple entry. Even if the temple entrance is away by few hundred meters in case of large ancient temples, there wouldn't be any disturbance in the middle to block the view of Linga. Usually it will be visible from outside of the temple. In some temples we can find a huge Nandi (Bull) which is considered as Shiva's vehicle. Actually Shiva doesn't need any vehicle because he has attained infiniteness. Ancient Hindus have kept a bull to show the order again. Since Shiva is represented as a male god, they have chosen the bull {Fig.19}, which is known for its aggressive male nature.

Fig.19 Nandi (The Bull)

Aggressiveness is an inherent quality of most of the male species in our existence. But if we observe the Nandi carefully, it will be sitting very calmly facing the Linga. Even though bull is aggressive, it has the same order like the Linga (body, mind and consciousness). In fact all the animals are in the same order and every animal knows the truth except man because of his intellect which separates him from truth. So, while entering the Shiva temple, one can look at the bull and try to understand that the one who is within us is also the one who is within the bull.

In some temples it is observed that a five headed Snake made of gold or silver is placed over the Linga as an ornament. Snake which represents the knowledge should be kept always on the second layer of the Linga. Nothing should be above the third layer of Linga which shows the infiniteness. That is the reason ancient Hindus who have designed the Linga didn't represent Linga with a snake. This overhead snake might have been added in later centuries by the people who were not aware of the actual meaning of Linga. Similarly so many things have been changed in recent years, due to artistic reasons and misinterpretation.

In most of the ancient Shiva temples we can find a small Vishnu temple at some corner within the temple complex but we won't find Shiva or Linga in any Vishnu temple. Reason is simple where there is mind (Vishnu) there can't be consciousness (Shiva) but where there is consciousness; mind will be there but kept aside in a place where it has to be. Mind should always be used as a weapon (Trident) as shown in {Fig.16} and used only when it is needed.

So this is the actual meaning of the representation of Trimurti, Creator, Protector and Destroyer (Brahma, Vishnu and Shiva) in Hinduism, which shows the evolution of man. All these are representations of body, mind and consciousness but not actually gods. So many Puranas and stories have been written for thousands of years, considering each one as god but all of them are imaginations.

Usually Shiva is shown as an ascetic but in some places he is depicted as a family man too because it is not necessary that one needs to renounce everything after liberation, one can even continue as a family man. Anyone can attain liberation irrespective of marital status.

One can perform all his prescribed duties and fulfil his family requirements without getting attached. That's the reason Shiva has also been represented as a family man. Here I would like to talk about some more ancient stories to explain further about Shiva. But it seems like these stories were added after the invention of Trimurti Gods. Instead of worrying about the time period when it has been conceived, I would like to explain the significance of these stories.

Shiva has been married to Parvathi {Fig.20}. She is considered as a universal mother and they have two sons Ganesha and Karthikeya. She is also represented in various forms but I have chosen a simple picture showing her in a standing posture with two bare hands. Here also, right hand shown above the left hand to depict that the right ear is sensitive than left ear. Almost most of the Hindu gods are represented in the same hand gesture for the same reason.

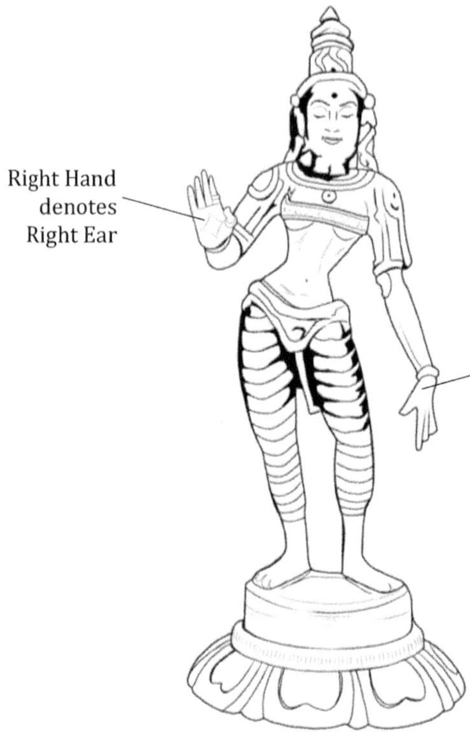

Fig.20 Goddess Parvathi

According to mythology, it is said that Ganesha has been made by Parvathi for her personal protection and has given him all her knowledge. Then she instructed Ganesha to act as her personal guard and prevent anyone from entering her place.

Later when Shiva (an awakened man) arrived to meet his wife Parvathi, he was stopped by Ganesha, who has received order from his mother to not to allow anyone. For all the questions Shiva asked, Ganesha replied it in a more intellectual way.

Angered by Ganesha's attitude, Shiva took his weapon (Trident) and severed Ganesha's head. Later when Parvathi came to know about this incident, she pleaded Shiva to get Ganesha back to life. So Shiva ordered other few gods to visit earth and bring the head of the first dead creature they see on earth. These gods came across a dead elephant and after so much of discussion they decided to take the head of the dead elephant. This head has been attached to Ganesha and he was brought back to life. After this Shiva declared Ganesha as a first god to be worshipped and from then he has been worshipped as a god with an elephant head. Even today in all Shiva temples, people worship Ganesha first at the entrance of the temple and then Karthikeya to respect Shiva's words.

Now let's look at the actual significance of the above incident. Mother (Parvathi) has created child (Ganesha) and has given him knowledge about worldly things and then he has become an intellectual. This happens to every child, the first source of knowledge or information about the world is always through the mother. She is the one who introduces even father to the child. An Intellectual (ego) thinks that he is the smartest, knowledgeable person in the world. But this knowledge has not come on its own; it has been transferred from one to another which is not perfect and always limited.

"What one considers as his intellect is a sum of accumulation of so many people's ideologies".

When Ganesha blocked Shiva and asked so many intellectual questions, Shiva got angry and he used his Trident (knowledge) and severed Ganesha's head which basically represents that he removed Ganesha's ego. It simply means that an awakened man's wisdom will remove the ignorance (ego) of the intellectual because wisdom means "knowing oneself" which the intellectual lacks.

Later his head has been replaced with elephant head to show that even though Elephant has such a big head with bigger brain; it doesn't have the ego like the one which man carries on his head. So after replacing with animal head Ganesha has attained liberation. It conveys,

"Unless an intellectual head is replaced with wisdom, it's impossible to know the Truth"

As mentioned earlier that all animals live in the moment and act instinctively except man who always lives in the past and future except the present. So to symbolically represent it, they have shown Ganesha {Fig.21} with an elephant head and he is known for his wisdom. His wisdom has been proved in 'Fruit of knowledge' story which I would like to explain later.

Fig.21 Ganesha

Ganesha is also represented in various forms with four hands like Vishnu. He holds a goad (sharper tool) on his upper right hand and noose (softer rope) on his upper left hand, which were positioned in line with the ears to represent the right and left cochlea of the ear and their difference. He is usually depicted with big belly and he holds rice balls in his lower left hand to show his gluttony. This has been given to show his wisdom because basic need of any man for his survival is food. After food whatever one struggles to achieve is because of his desire or passion which arises from the mind and it eventually leads to suffering. Here I would like to mention Zen master "Linji Yixuan" saying, ***"When hungry, eat your rice; when tired, close your eyes. Fools may laugh at me but wise men will know what I mean".***

Mouse which is known for its intelligence is depicted as his vehicle. Another noticeable aspect of Ganesha is the difference in the length of the tusk. His left tusk is shown shorter than the right one. There are different versions of stories told about his broken left tusk. In one version Parasurama (6th incarnation of Vishnu) went to meet Shiva but he was blocked by Ganesha which led to tussle between both. Parasurama hurled his axe on Ganesha out of anger; Ganesha who knows that the axe was given by his father (Shiva) to Parasurama took a blow on his left tusk to show his respect for his father. In another version it is said that he broke his left tusk to write Mahabharata. But his shorter left tusk is actually to depict that he has attained liberation.

Now let's know about Ganesha's brother Karthikeya. As per mythology, Karthikeya {Fig.22} is the younger son of Shiva and he was created to destroy the demons on earth and save people. Parvathi (mother) has given him a weapon called as Vel (spear) which symbolically represents knowledge. Instead of showing the ears and brain as distinctive figure like in Trident, here it is combined into one to form a Spear and the shaft represents the spinal cord.

Fig.22 Karthikeya

Karthikeya is also called as six faced God to denote that he is the sixth sense and peacock is shown as his vehicle to represent that the knowledge (sound) travels in the air. He is predominantly worshipped in south India and all his six temples are located in Tamil Nadu. There is a doubt among people that whether some of the Karthikeya temples were converted into

Vishnu Temples because, both of them are represented with two wives and both has bird as their vehicles, even the way they stand also looks almost similar. But the main reason is, both Vishnu and Karthikeya represents mind. Two wives of Karthikeya are to show two ears {Fig.23}, it can be clearly understood through their standing posture with their hands positioned away from their body to symbolically represent the ear curvature. They have also shown the difference between the ears by naming the right ear as Valli and left ear as Deivanai. We can see the similar representation of Vishnu with his two wives Sridevi and Bhoodevi in {Fig.24}. This representation is to show that sound enters through the ears and develops as sixth sense, but this has been wrongly conveyed as God with two wives. The reason for this difference between the ears has been explained clearly in {Sec.6.2}.

Fig.23 Karthikeya with his Two Wives

Fig.24 Vishnu with his Two Wives

Let's see the story of fruit of knowledge, as per mythology Narada (sage) brought a fruit of knowledge to Shiva. Shiva who knows the ultimate truth doesn't need any other knowledge, so he decided to give it to his sons. Shiva being a wise man decided to cut it into two halves and give it to both of his sons but Narada stopped him from doing it by citing it shouldn't be divided. So there was confusion, to whom it has to be offered among Ganesha and Karthikeya. Again Narada gave an idea to give the fruit of knowledge to the one who comes first after circumambulating the world thrice. After hearing this, Karthikeya (Sixth sense) immediately sat on his peacock and started circumambulating the world. But Ganesha being wise thought that for a child the world is nothing more than its father and mother. So he circumambulated Shiva and Parvathi thrice and took the fruit. When Karthikeya came back after completing his task, he came to know that he was defeated by his wiser brother and felt ashamed for his ignorance. Later he left everything and stood naked (Nirvana) on a hill in Palani (place in Tamil Nadu) to know himself.

This story is again to show the actual wisdom. As per intellectual understanding world means literally our planet. So Karthikeya being sixth sense (mind) decided to travel around the world but Ganesha who has been liberated by Shiva, understood that for a child, world means the knowledge it has received (heard) from its mother and father. So he decided that by circumambulating around his father and mother is equivalent as travelling around the world and pleased everyone and won the fruit of knowledge. This is wisdom because in reality the world which one perceives is totally based on the ideas and concepts given by others, nothing is inherent in fact the only inherent thing is nothingness which one realizes after enlightenment and this nothingness is wholeness.

This is how the stories have been created to explain how the man evolves. Initially they worshipped the impersonal Brahman and then they have given the form of Linga and then again divided the Linga into trinity. Brahma, Vishnu and Shiva and assigned each one of them with different job of creation, preservation and destruction to denote the body, mind and consciousness. Later so many other stories and other forms of gods have been introduced but all of them are representation of body and mind. Among male gods consciousness has been represented only by Shiva (Self- realized man) with a wisdom eye opened.

6.4 Nataraja

Fig.25 Nataraja (Supreme Being)

With this understanding now we explore the actual meaning of cosmic dance Nataraja. As I have already mentioned that Nataraja {Fig.25} is the representation of cosmic consciousness (Brahman). It is the only statue, where they have represented the formless in a form, that's why they made it into dance instead of a standing posture to show it is the cause of all the changes. If one has carefully observed all the gods which are representation of mind like Vishnu, Lakshmi, Parvathi and Karthikeya, they are represented as standing on half lotus but in Nataraja, he is shown as dancing over the small demon on the lotus base. The name of the dwarf under his feet is called Muyalakan (knowledge).

Nataraja keeps his right foot over Muyalakan and raises his left foot in air in a dancing posture, but Muyalakan is not killed because if he dies then there wouldn't be knowledge in the world. He is also depicted as holding Damaru in his upper right hand and fire in his upper left hand and two lower hands are shown as a sign of blessing.

Actual significance of this statue is the lotus base on which Nataraja dances is nothing but the representation of the right and left hemisphere of our brain as shown in {Fig.26}. Ancient Hindus have accurately located on which side of our brain is our intellect which is responsible for our ignorance.

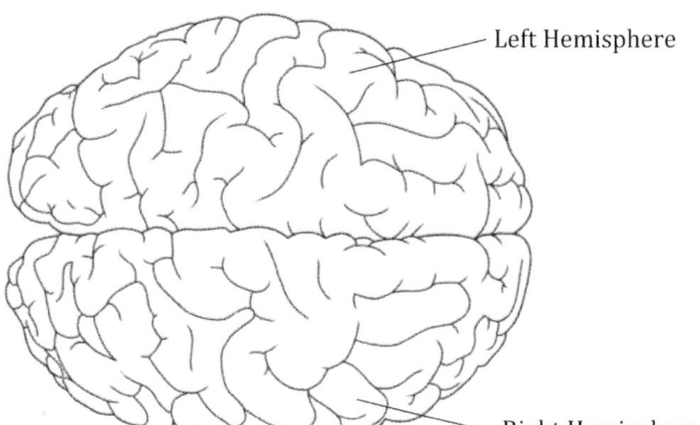

Fig.26 Top view of Human Brain

We have already seen that Vishnu's chakra (Disc) represents the cochlea of the right ear. In mythological stories, he uses this

Disc (chakra) to kill the demons, which means to make one unconscious of his nature by imparting knowledge. This knowledge is the cause of one's ignorance, one's forgetfulness about the Self and one's false identification with the ego. As we have already seen how knowledge develops by hearing the sound. This sound is the basis for any language and science has confirmed that the left hemisphere of the brain is language dominant area. Also within the left hemisphere there are certain regions which are playing a vital role when it comes to language comprehension (Friederici, 2011). Most important among them is superior temporal gyrus which is located just above the left ear. This superior temporal gyrus which consists of Primary and secondary auditory cortex along with Wernicke's area of temporal lobe in the left hemisphere has been pulled out and shown as Muyalakan {Fig.27} and this is the place where one hears the eternal song of the Supreme Being Brahman after enlightenment.

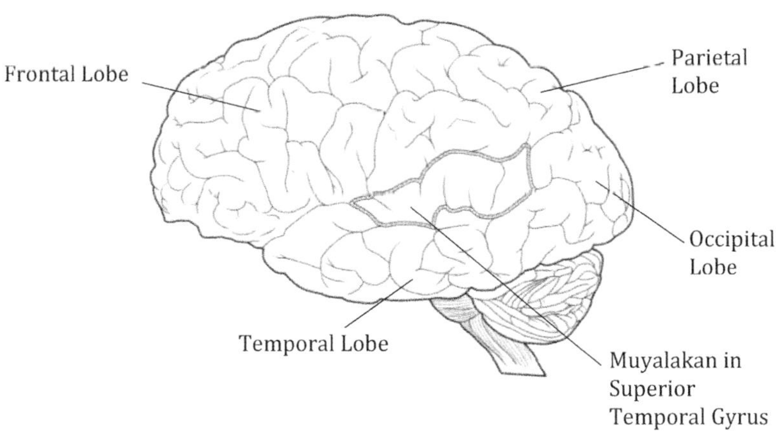

Fig.27 Left hemisphere of the Brain

Basically mind is the one which gives the perception of an individual ego, by continuously generating thoughts about the past and future. When one stop thinking, he lives in the now moment. So what is thinking, it is creating a thought, let's understand the foundation of thought. Thought is basically an unspoken sentences running inside the head. To form a thought one must know a particular language. If one doesn't know any language one can't think at all. This is what happens with newborns they can't think because they don't know the language to create a thought. So the basis of a thought is language which is very vital to frame a sentence and the foundation of the language is sound. Hinduism has perfectly identified that the mind develops by hearing the language as sounds. That's why all the gods who represents mind are depicted with a weapon which symbolises the cochlea of the ears which is the vital organ of hearing. So the language is the one which creates the world around, by naming the objects around or by assigning them with different sounds. This same language is the reason for introducing the concept of classifying something as subject (I) and something or someone else as object. In simple terms language introduces the concept of duality. As soon as one starts classifying everything around, it also starts creating illusion that "I" as a separate entity. So language is the cause for development of the mind. Once the mind develops it keeps one under its control by creating thought, it always gives the perception of duality 'I' as a subject and everything else as an object. When one attains liberation, one starts listening to the sound of the Supreme Being on the left hemisphere of the brain, through which it suppresses the mind which creates thoughts. When the thoughts disappears naturally one's identity with the mind also disappears, which makes one to experience the Self and existence as one which is called as oneness or Samadhi.

"Duality is an illusion which exists only in the mind and not in reality".

So Nataraja by keeping his right foot over the left hemisphere of the brain and with his left foot in air denotes that when the Brahman arrives, it suppresses the mind and gives liberation, because killing the mind damages the temporal lobe which leads to memory loss so Nataraja just suppresses the mind, so that mind will be available to use when required. The Damaru in his upper right hand is meant to show that Supreme Being is a soundless sound. Fire in the upper left hand shows that he is the source of everything and the two lower hands represents liberation. This is the actual meaning of Nataraja. They have tried to represent Enlightenment through a statue. It is very surprising to realize that how someone can give such a detailed scientific graphical representation for Enlightenment. This is Hinduism; they have mastered the anatomy of human body and represented everything as a sculpture or statue instead of saying or writing it directly. As I mentioned earlier everything is representation and not actual god because the Supreme Being Brahman is formless and it's beyond human intelligence to comprehend about its characteristics. This representation of Supreme Being as Nataraja statue is just a mental speculation.

When one attains enlightenment he will be absorbed into the existence by the soundless sound of the Supreme Being. In fact everyone is part of existence but the egoic mind is the reason behind our forgetfulness, which the sound of the supreme being suppresses and makes one to live in the present moment. People who are considering enlightenment as just a psychological transformation are missing the vital part of the change, because what they are observing as change is the effect on someone's brain but they fail to analyse the cause behind the transformation. It can never be analysed because it is beyond analysis.

I would like to give a short summary about what we have discussed so far in this chapter. God the Supreme Being in Hinduism is formless and it is called as Brahman (cosmic consciousness). This Brahman is expressing itself in various forms like a fish, a tree, a bird, an animal and also as a human being. Realizing this Brahman in one's Self (soul) is called liberation or Moksha. As it has become difficult to perceive the impersonal god, ancestors have introduced the concept of Trimurti as Brahma, Vishnu and Shiva and assigned each one with a role as a creator, protector and destroyer. These three gods are nothing but the three layers of man, body, mind and consciousness. Brahma with his four heads and single body represents the body with five senses. Vishnu has been shown as ear passage, with his weapons (Disc and conchshell) representing the cochlea of the ear and by connecting him to Brahma's lotus, they have shown the connection of ear to brain. So Vishnu is the sixth sense (mind) which develops by hearing the sound through ears and registering as a memory in the brain. Brahma has been called as God of creation and Vishnu has been called as the god of protection to show that the Body (Brahma) creates this materialistic world under the instruction of Mind (Vishnu). Knowledge covers one's wisdom eye and makes one forget his original nature by identifying himself with the mind. But when he meditates and realizes his Self (consciousness), his wisdom eye opens which destroys the illusionary materialistic world and he attains liberation. So the Self-realized man has been called as Shiva (god of destroyer). Every man is Brahma and Vishnu together and there is potential to turn himself into a Shiva. Also we have seen the meaning of representation of consorts of Trimurti and Shiva's sons Ganesha and Karthikeya. Finally the cosmic dance Nataraja is the representation of

Supreme being (cosmic consciousness) which has been depicted as dancing over the left hemisphere of the brain by which it suppresses the mind and gives liberation.

7 Sects within Hinduism

As we have seen in the previous chapter that evolution of man has been represented with all male Gods. So in the later stage they also started to represent it through female gods, again with various stories to support that particular form. Also so many gods which have been conceived and worshipped by tribes and aboriginals were brought under the broad umbrella of Hinduism through puranic stories. This is how the number of Gods has increased in Hinduism. The actual representation of Gods has been hidden and people continued to worship the dieties which their ancestors has worshipped. Those who worshipped Shiva were called as following Shaivism and those worshipped Vishnu were called as following Vaishnavism and those who worshipped female forms of gods were called as following Shaktism. These divisions of sects within Hinduism has led to creation of so many stories for the deity which they worshipped, inorder to project their favourite deity as supreme than all other deities.

Especially Vaishnavism, who knew that they are worshipping mind, which is below consciousness, has represented Vishnu in so many incarnations (avatars) in order to represent how the mind develops in a man. As mind (Vishnu) cannot come directly which is formless and also an illusion, they created so many avatars to personify mind. But all of them are mind and not consciousness. Through these avatars which are very evident in many of the stories, they brought Shiva below Vishnu to show the domination of mind over consciousness. Some of the well known avatars are Matsya, Kurma, Varaha, Narasimha, Vamana, Parasurama, Rama, Krishna, Balarama and Kalki {Fig.28}.

Fig.28 Dasavatharam of Vishnu

Let's have a look at these avatars briefly and understand what they convey actually.

7.1 Matsya Avatar

According to mythology the first incarnation or avatar is said to be a Fish (Matsya). It is said that Vishnu appeared as a fish and warned about the great flood and preserved human beings and other creatures from danger. In other version of story it is said that he took the form of fish and saved the Vedas. This form is usually represented as half fish and half human, which represents the typical Vishnu with his four hands {Fig.29}.

I have already mentioned that Vishnu is a sound. Sound is basically a wave with crest and trough which carries information about certain object or action, attributes or event. These waves are same like waves of an Ocean. That's why Vishnu has been represented as a fish, a creature which lives in the ocean to symbolise that the information is carried by the sound waves.

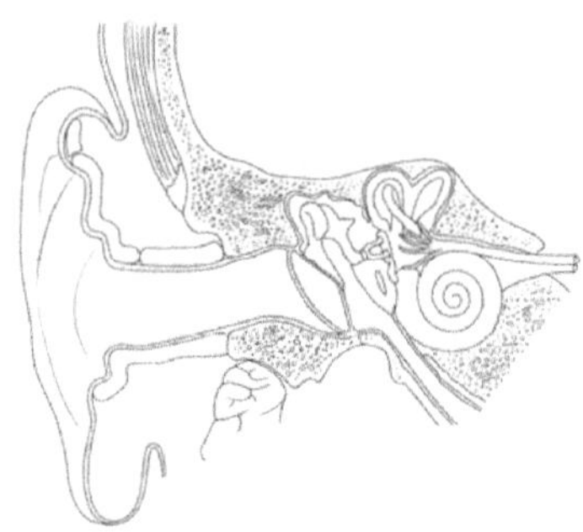

Sound Wave Entering Ear

Matsya

Fig.29 Sound Wave as Matsya Avatar

7.2 Kurma Avatar

The second avatar is Kurma (Tortoise). In this avatar, it is said that gods and demons churned the ocean of milk in order to get the Amrita (nectar), which gives immortality. They used a serpent called Vasuki as rope and a mountain called Mandara as churning stick. As the mount Mandara started drowning inside the ocean, Vishnu took the form of tortoise and supported the mount with his shell. This form has been depicted as half tortoise and half human which represents Vishnu with his weapons.

But the actual meaning is, once the sound waves enter the auditory passage of the ear, it hits the tympanic membrane or ear drum, which looks like a tortoise shell. This membrane is positioned in such a way that it lifts the sound wave from surface of the auditory passage and passes it to the middle ear region {Fig.30}. This tympanic membrane has been depicted as a tortoise, second form of Vishnu (incarnation) with such a vast story and so many descriptions and characters.

Kurma Ear Drum

Fig.30 Ear Drum as Kurma Avatar

7.3 Varaha Avatar

Next Vishnu took the form of Varaha (Boar) to save earth from a demon called Hiranyaksha. This demon prayed to Brahma and got a boon that no god or demon or any animal can kill him. With this boon he started torturing people in the world and he took the earth to the underworld and submerged it in the ocean. So all other gods prayed to Brahma and asked him to save earth from the disaster, Brahma in-turn prayed to Vishnu. Then a small creature has fallen from Brahma's nostril and it took the form of giant boar {Fig.31}, because Hiranyaksha has left the name of boar while asking boon from Brahma. So Vishnu used this loop hole in Brahma's boon as an advantage and appeared in the form of boar and lifted the earth from the bottom of ocean with its tusk and killed Hiranyaksha. The actual meaning is, once the sound passes from tympanic membrane; it hits the three oscillatory bones (Malleus, Incus and Stapes) and reaches the inner ear region. Of this three bones structure the first two structures (Malleus and Incus) has been depicted as third incarnation of Vishnu as a boar with its tusk. It seems like just to represent the Malleus and Incus of the middle ear in the form of boar, Brahma has given the boon to Hiranyaksha excluding the boar.

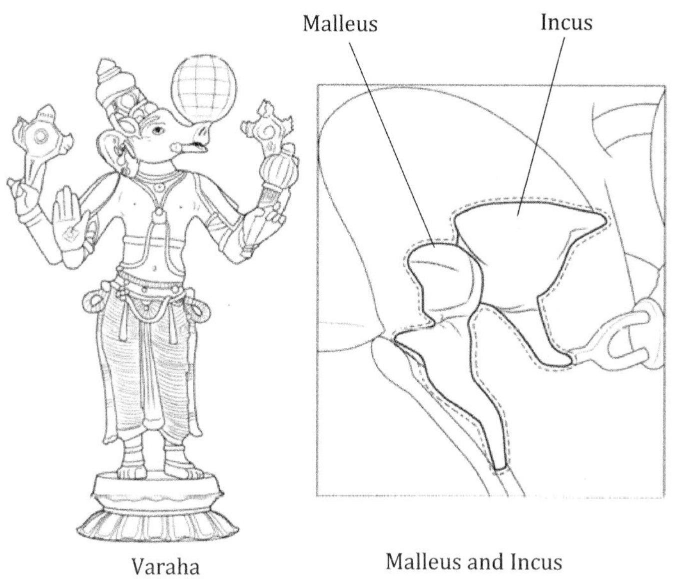

Fig.31 Malleus and Incus as Varaha Avatar

7.4 Narasimha Avatar

Next avatar is Narasimha avatar or half lion incarnation. In Varaha avatar, Vishnu killed demon Hiranyaksha by incarnating in the form of boar. This incident angered his brother Hiranyakashipu, so he wanted to take revenge on Vishnu. He meditated to Brahma and got a boon that no one could be able to kill him either in day or night, inside or outside, either by man or animal and by any weapon. With this boon he started ruling the world by claiming himself as god, but his son Prahlada who is firm believer of Vishnu didn't accept him as a god. So Hiranyakashipu tried to kill his own son by throwing him into fire, offering him to venomous snakes and so on but everytime Prahlada was saved by Vishnu. Hiranyakashipu finally lost his patience and asked his son that where is your God (Vishnu)? Prahlada replied that God lives everywhere even in the dust and in the pillars. Then Hiranyakashipu took his club and broke the pillar next to him to prove that his son is wrong. But from the pillar there emerged a strange creature with torso of man and head of lion, again Vishnu used the loophole in Brahma's boon and appeared as Narasimha {Fig.32}. He took Hiranyakashipu on his lap and torn the stomach and took out the intestine with his sharp nails in the twilight and killed him.

The actual meaning is when the sound passes from Malleus and Incus; it reaches the Stapes, a very important structure which passes the sound into the inner ear region through the oval window. This stapes has been depicted as club breaking the pillar and the semicircular canals along with vestibule has been depicted as Narasimha tearing the body of Hiranyakashipu. So in the fourth avatar they have covered the organs of the ear starting from auditory passage to semicircular canals of the vestibular membrane.

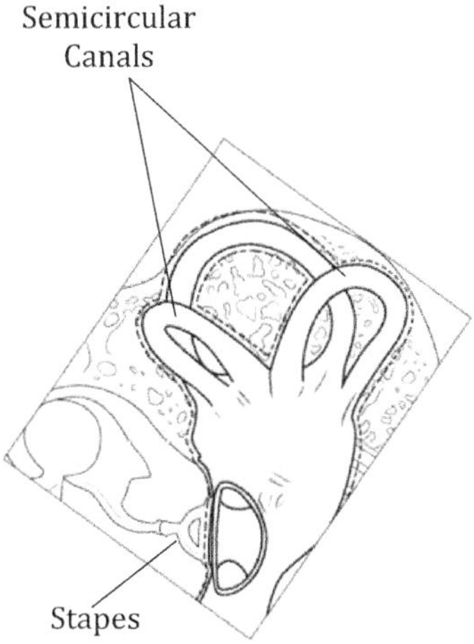

Narasimha

Semicircular Canals

Fig.32 Semicircular Canals as Narasimha Avatar

They tried to represent the journey of sound within the ear by personifying each organ as an avatar or incarnation. Gradually from animal form they have moved to human form in the Fifth avatar which is Vamana or dwarf man {Fig.33}.

7.5 Vamana Avatar

As per the story, King Bali who was the grandson of Prahlada performed a penance and got a boon from Brahma (creator), that no one can defeat him in any battle in any world. With this boon he conquered all the three worlds and dethroned all the Gods who were ruling the heaven, but he was a noble person and he didn't trouble anyone. So people were naturally happy with his monarchy. But Indra, the ruler of heaven who was upset about his loss of heavenly kingdom, grieved to Aditi (mother of Gods). Aditi in turn performed a penance to please Vishnu and asked him to recover the heaven and give back to Indra. Then Vishnu appeared in the form of Vamana on the auspicious day when Bali was performing a yagna (sacrificial ceremony) to offer anything to anyone as per their wish. Vamana came with an Umbrella and Kamandala (vessel to carry water) and asked Bali for three feet of land measured by his own foot. King Bali even though recognised that Vishnu has come in the form of dwarf (Vamana) but agreed and offered him the land. Immediately after the offer, Vamana took the form of giant and expanded into the cosmos and measured the whole earth with his first feet and entire universe with his second feet and asked King Bali where to put his third feet. The humble king told him to put the third feet on his head. So Vamana kept the third feet on his head and sent him into the underworld, but he was blessed with immortality to rule the underworld forever.

The actual meaning is, once the sound passes through the stapes and vestibule, it reaches the cochlea, an important organ which converts the sound waves into electrical impulses based on the vibration of the hair cells within it. Cochlea is approximately 30mm long and coiled 2.75 times in its horizontal axis (Rask-Andersen, et al., 2012) (Hardy, 1938). In the last chapter, we have seen the detailed cross section and function of cochlea {Fig.7} and it is the one which has been represented as Vishnu's weapon on two sides of the ears as chakra (Disc) and conchshell. Here Vamana has been mentioned as asking for 3 feet of land is to specify the number of turns of cochlea. It is indirectly conveyed that cochlea is coiled 2.75 times, so to complete the third it has to reach the brain which is head. Even though cochlea looks like a small structure it plays a crucial role in hearing. This is the actual meaning behind this whole story. Vamana has been represented as carrying a Kamandala filled with water in one hand and an umbrella in other hand to show the connection between cochlea and brain.

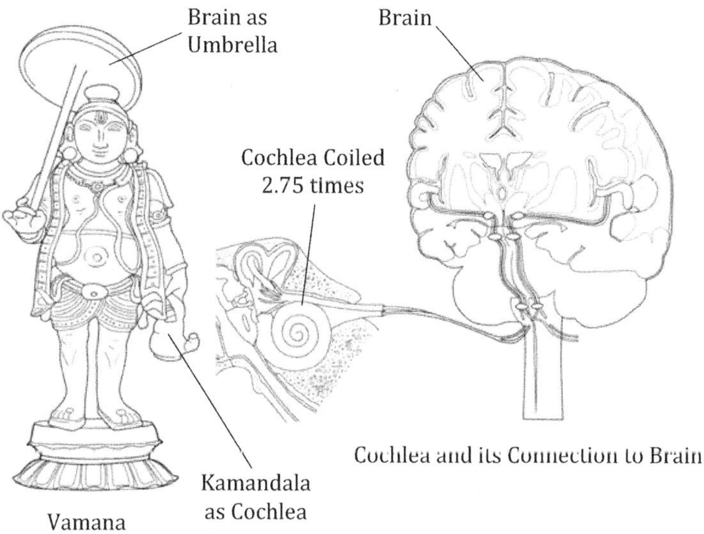

Fig.33 Cochlea as Vamana Avatar

Through the first five avatars they have depicted how sound travels through each organ and reach the brain. Since they have represented each organ inside the ear separately as an avatar, from the sixth incarnation they introduced sound in human form and through series of events in their life they tried to represent the sound travelling through each ear separately and reaching the brain.

7.6 Parasurama Avatar

Sixth avatar is Parasurama {Fig.34}. He was said to be born as Brahmana (the learned one) but he had the qualities of Kshatriya (the warrior). He was represented as holding an axe in his right hand and was known for his short temper.

His father was killed by a Kshatriya king when he refused to donate his holy cow (kamadhenu). He has taken the oath to kill all the Kshatriya kings in the world to take revenge for his father's death. He found 21 scars on his father's body, so he travelled around the world 21 times and killed all Kshatriya's clan. He remained angry until he met the next incarnation Rama (a Kshatriya Prince) and then he calmed down and decided to meditate. He was said to be immortal and he even appeared in Krishna avatar.

Through series of events in his life they have tried to show again the sound travelling through the whole right ear till the brain. As we have already seen that cochlea of the right ear has been represented as Vishnu's chakra on the right hand to show the sharpness of the right ear over the left ear. For the same reason Parasurama has been shown holding an axe in his right hand. The surface area ratio of ear drum to the oval window is (20/1), this helps in amplifying the sound and resonate the hair cells in the inner ear (Blatrix & Mondain, 2020). This information has been conveyed as he travelled around the world 21 times. So this is how they have mentioned so many minute details in every avatar and shown the development of mind.

Fig.34 Parasurama as Sixth Avatar

7.7 Rama Avatar

The next avatar is Rama (the perfect man). His life story has been narrated through the great Epic Ramayana. He has been depicted as the Kshatriya prince and married to Sita. He was sent to Vanavasa (exile in forest) for 14 years because of his step mother's plot. His wife Sita and his brother Lakshmana also decided to accompany him during the period of exile. During that period, Shurpanakha the sister of Ravana (ruler of Sri Lanka), got impressed by Rama's beauty and asked him to marry her. But Rama rejected her by saying that he was already married to beautiful Sita. Then she approached Lakshmana, Lakshmana also rejected her. This incident made her angry, so she tried to hurt Sita, this made Lakshmana angry and he cut the nose and left ear of Shurpanakha. To take revenge for this act, Shurpanakha went back to Sri Lanka and informed Ravana about Sita and told him to abduct Sita and marry her. Ravana arrived in the jungle where the trio were staying and instructed his uncle Marich to transform into a golden deer and grab the attention of Sita. As expected Sita liked the golden deer and wanted it. To fulfill Sita's wish Rama went to hunt the deer, and he shot the deer with his arrow. When the deer was about to die, it mimicked in Rama's voice and shouted for help. On hearing Rama's voice, Sita told Lakshmana to check what happened to Rama. Lakshmana drew a line around the hut and told Sita not to cross the line in any circumstances until he is back. Ravana who was watching this entire scene appeared like an ascetic and told Sita to cross the line and offer him food. The moment she crossed, he kidnapped Sita and took her to Sri Lanka in his Pushpaka Vimana (aeroplane). This incident took Rama into deep grieve. Later he met Hanuman, who has taken him to the monkey King Sugriva, who was also suffering like Rama by losing his wife and wealth to his brother Vaali. Rama promised to help Sugriva to recover his kingdom and wife from vaali. Vaali has a special power, if anyone comes in front of him to fight, he will take half of the opponent's power and becomes even more powerful. So Rama suggested Sugriva to wear a garland and fight with his brother Vaali because Vaali and Sugriva were identical twins. While they were fighting, Rama by hiding behind the tree shot an arrow on Vaali and killed him. Later Hanuman flew to Sri Lanka and met Sita and gave Rama's ring. He conveyed Rama's message to Ravana to release Sita but when Ravana didn't respect it, Hanuman created turbulence in Sri Lanka to show

Rama's power. Meanwhile Ravana's brother Vibhishana, who didn't like abducting Sita, helped Rama and shared Ravana's important military secrets. Then Sugriva along with Hanuman helped Rama in constructing the bridge from Rameshwaram to Sri Lanka and fought with Ravana's army. During the war Lakshmana got injured and to cure it, Hanuman went thousands of miles away and took an entire mountain called Dronagiri on his right palm which has secret herb to heal the wound. Once Lakshmana was healed, Rama killed Ravana and returned to Ayodhya along with Sita.

Through various incidents they tried to show the mercy of Rama, he had bigger heart even to forgive Ravana. But the complete story was made to show the sound entering through the left ear from auditory passage to right brain. This has been depicted by Rama holding a bow on his left hand {Fig.35} and by Hanuman carrying mountain on his right palm. As we already know that the left ear has been represented as conchshell in Vishnu's hands to show its mildness and differentiate it from the right ear. Rama's character has been portrayed as a mild mannered and soft spoken person to differentiate him from Parasurama, who represents the sound in right ear. For the same reason they have created an interaction between Rama and Parasurama and only after this interaction Parasurama realized that Rama was his mirror image and calmed down.

As we know, for mind to develop it has to hear sounds from both the ears and has to reach both hemispheres of the brain. This has been made into a very big story and made more realistic by including so many real geographical information.

Recent studies on neuroscience are showing stronger evidence that both the hemispheres of the brain collaborate and interact with each other through Corpus callosum when it comes to language comprehension (Cook, 2002). The left hemisphere of the brain is more involved in semantics (understanding the meaning of the word) and syntax processing (structure of sentences) while right hemisphere is involved in prosodic processing (decoding the acoustic part of the speech like tone, rhythm and pitch) (Friederici & Alter, 2004) (Bryan, 1989).

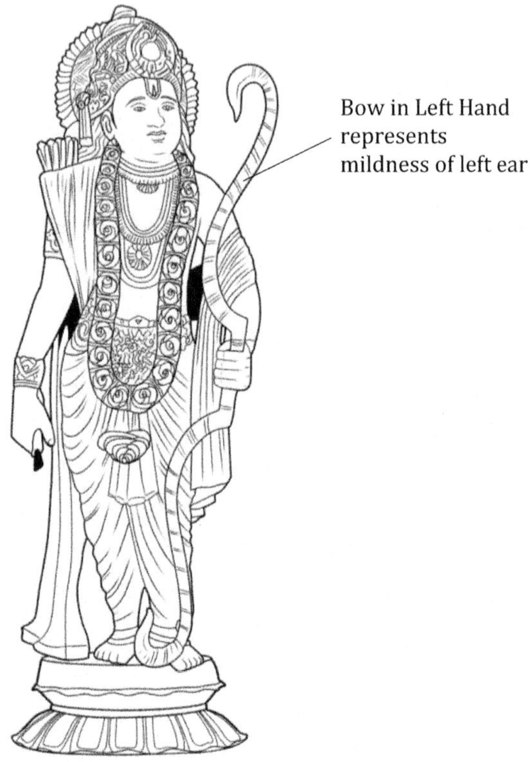

Fig.35 Rama as Seventh Avatar

7.8 Krishna Avatar

Fig.36 Krishna as Eight Avatar

Next eighth avatar is Krishna avatar {Fig.36}. He has been hailed as complete avatar because in the first five avatars they introduced the organs inside the ear in the sequence to show how the sound enters and reaches the brain and in the sixth and seventh avatars they have personified sound into man with various qualities and life events to depict the sound travelling through right and left ear separately and through their interaction they have shown how the mind evolves. Also both Parasurama and Rama worshipped Shiva to show that they were mind and the order of body, mind and consciousness has been maintained till seventh avatar. But in Krishna avatar, they have shown how the mind develops and overtakes consciousness. Another reason might be that until the age of seven, children are poor at comprehending structurally complex sentences even though they have the capability to comprehend simple sentences perfectly. It is mainly attributed due to the immaturity of language network areas within the left hemispheres (Friederici, Brauer, & Lohman, 2011).

Also we have discussed in detail, the anatomy of the human ear and how sound travels inside the ear through various organs and finally reaches brain. I recommend readers to watch videos of anatomy of ear in detail for better understanding.

There were so many stories told about Krishna right from his birth to Kurukshetra war but all these stories were made to explain how the mind develops. Let's take a look at some of the stories of Krishna right from his birth.

It needs another book to write the stories of Krishna in detail but my intention is to convey the actual meaning rather than explaining the stories with so many characters. As we have seen in the first five avatars, how a vast story with so many characters were introduced, just to represent the minute organs inside the ear.

Krishna was born as the eighth child to his Parents, which denote the eighth nerve (vestibulocochlear nerve) which is responsible for hearing. Later when Krishna was born, it is mentioned that he has born in his original form with four hands holding Chakra and conchshell in the upper hands and club (Gadha) and lotus in the lower hands, which is typical representation of Vishnu (mind) which we have seen in the previous chapters and their meanings. Later Krishna's parents requested him to change into normal form then he transformed into a small child.

Fig.37 Balarama as Ninth Avatar

There were some incidents of baby Krishna killing demon and breaking the cart but the most interesting events comes when he had grown up. Balarama (ninth incarnation) {Fig.37} had accompanied Krishna in most of the incidents. He was considered as an incarnation of Adishesha (the serpent). In an incident, Krishna was playing with his brother Balarama by holding the tail of cow. This incident depicts the sound passing from the ear drum to the three bones in the middle ear (Malleus, Incus and Stapes) {Fig.38}. Here the Malleus and Incus were together portrayed as a cow.

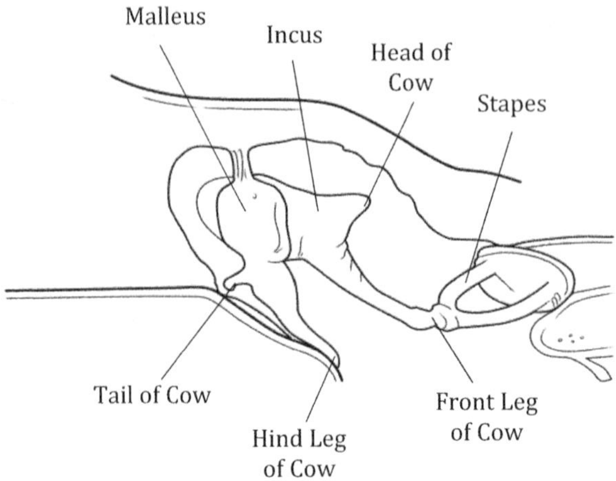

Fig.38 Krishna and Balarama Playing with Cow which represents sound passing through Middle Ear

So once the sound reaches the inner ear it has to pass through the cochlea, the coiled chamber which is filled with silvery grey coloured sodium and potassium rich fluids {Fig.7}. These fluids has been morphed as butter and yoghurt and said to be liked by Krishna. This incident has been depicted as Krishna stealing yoghurt and butter from neighbours (Gopis) and Gopis complaining to his mother about his mischief.

In another incident his Mother Yasodha chased Krishna to punish him for his mischief, which again to show the sound entering through the Malleus and Incus {Fig.39}, Where the Malleus and Incus has been portrayed as Yasodha leaning forward with hands stretched to catch Krishna.

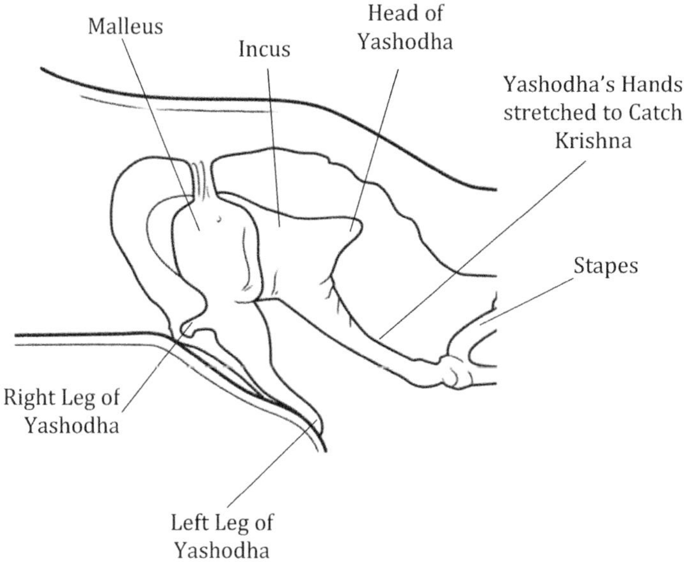

Fig.39 Yasodha chasing Krishna which represents Sound Passing through Malleus and Incus

Later she caught Krishna and tried to tie him to the wooden mortar but she found that the rope was less by two feet {Fig.40} and again she brought another longer rope which was also found to be less by two feet, after so many trails finally she managed to tie him. Here the Stapes (looks like a horse shoe) which takes sound to inner ear has been described as Wooden mortar and the two feet of rope has been mentioned to denote the two half rings of the stapes.

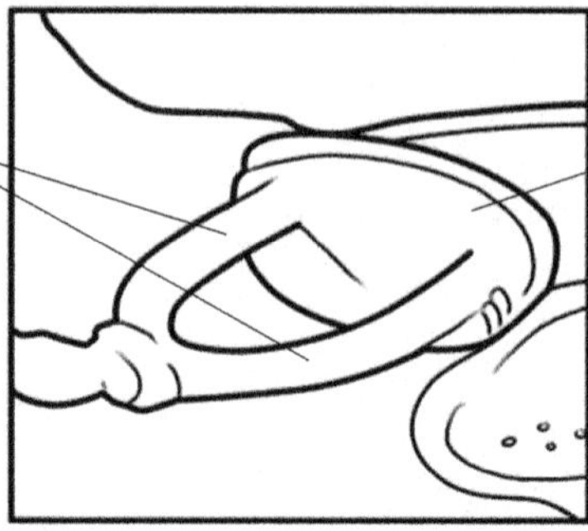

Fig.40 Krishna tied to Wooden Mortar which represents Stapes

After he was tied to the wooden mortar, he went in between two Arjuna trees and uprooted them and said to have given salvation for two sons of Kuvera called Nalakuvara and Manigriva. These two trees described as two gods are the semicircular canals of the inner ear {Fig.41}.

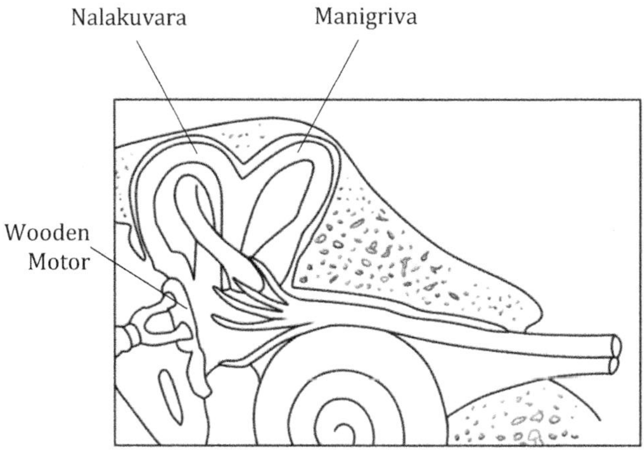

Fig.41 Krishna Liberating Kuvera's Sons which represents the Semicircular Canals of the Ear

Then there arrived an another demon called Bakasura in the form of huge bird with sharp beak and swallowed Krishna but Krishna came out from its mouth and killed the demon by tearing its beak into two parts. This incident is again to show the sound transferring from stapes and its connection to the inner ear region. In {Fig.42}, the opening of the oval window which connects the stapes to inner ear has been described as the mouth of the bird and semicircular canals were described as wings of the bird (Bakasura).

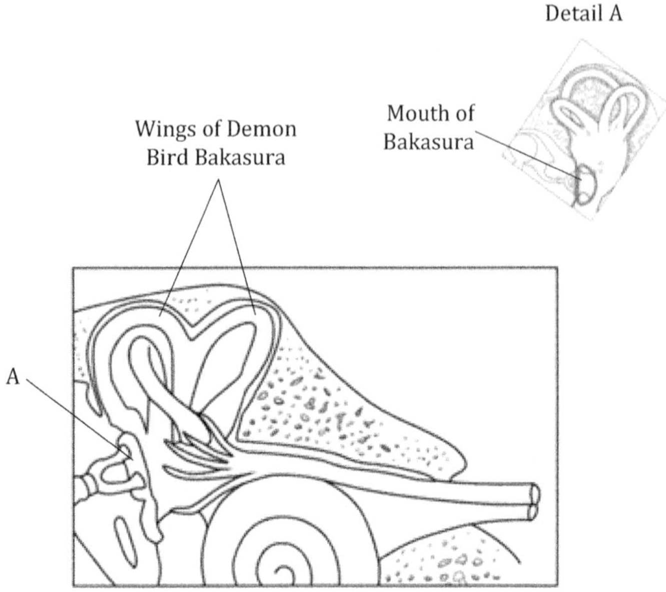

Fig.42 Krishna Fighting with Bakasura which represents Stapes and Semicircular Canals of the Ear

In another incident, a serpent called Aghasura with its wide opened mouth extended its body up to 8 miles long in order to kill Krishna {Fig.43}. Unknowingly Balarama along with his cowherd friends and calves entered into the mouth of the serpent Aghasura but Krishna killed the serpent and saved cows and cowherd boys. This incident was said to astonish even Brahma. In this incident, Cochlea of the ear is represented as a serpent and the cochlear nerve is the eighth nerve which represents the length of the serpent.

So after this incident Brahma (the creator god) kidnapped all those cow herd boys and calves to test Krishna's power but Krishna expanded himself into the forms of all his friends and calves and confused Brahma. After watching this incident, Brahma surrendered to Krishna. This clearly shows that once the sound passes through cochlea, it gets amplified into electrical signal by the hair cells within the cochlea and reaches the brain which is usually represented as lotus where the Brahma sits {Fig.9}. So Brahma has been brought into picture to show the arrival of the sound to the brain. This is how so many stories has been created to show how the sound travels through the ear by depicting each organ sometimes as demon or tree or various animals to indirectly convey that Knowledge is the sound and mind develops by hearing the sound.

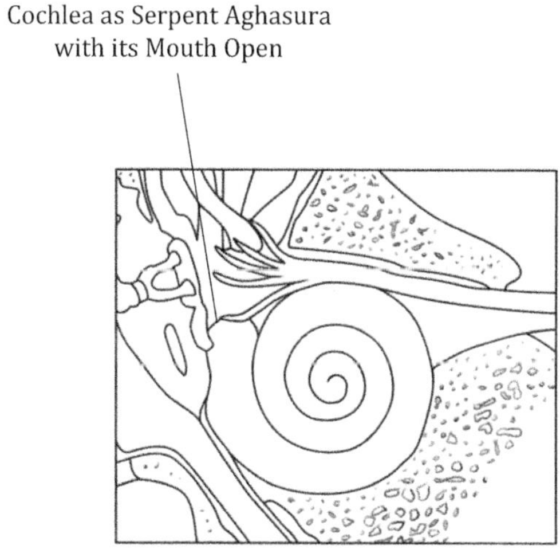

Fig.43 Cochlea which represents Aghasura (a Serpent)

Some of other incidents are Krishna and Balarama killing Dhenukasura, Krishna dancing on head of Kaliya (serpent), Balarama killing Pralambasura, Krishna lifting Govardhan hill were all again to show the same sound travelling through ear and reaching the brain. It is said that Krishna lifted the Govardhan hill at the age of seven and stood for seven days, here the brain has been represented as hill. As we have already seen that the Neuroscience studies shows stronger evidence that children's brain is not capable to process complex syntax (structural sentences) before the age of seven.

One of the very famous Krishna leela was Krishna dancing with Gopi's which is called as Rasa dance. It has been mentioned that around 16,000 Gopis have danced with Krishna.

In another very stunning and unbelievable story, Krishna fought with a demon called Bhaumasura and released 16,000 princesses who were kidnapped by him and later Krishna married all the 16,000 princesses. This number is exactly the number of hair cells (Michael-Titus, Revest, & Shortland, 2010) inside the cochlea of the ear and these hair cells are responsible for converting the sound into electrical impulses. When sound passes through the cochlea it touches all these hair cells before reaching the brain. So all these hair cells are represented as wives of Krishna. This is the actual reason behind Krishna having 16,000 wives and also his simultaneous expansion and dance with 16,000 Gopis. These hair cells are in the size of microns. How the Vedic people have managed to study these structures with such an accuracy to estimate it to exact value before the invention of high resolution microscopes is very surprising. This shows they were one of the most highly advanced human societies.

These stories of Krishna's past times are one of the most creative stories ever made in the history of mankind. Because such tiny organs inside the ear were described as an animal or a tree or a demon with such an enormous description to make it appear very realistic.

Usually Krishna has been depicted as playing a musical instrument (flute), which was given to him to clearly show that he is the sound (knowledge). As we have seen earlier Saraswathi (Goddess of knowledge) with musical instrument (Veena) and also Sanskrit is a sound which has been transferred through the ears in ancient times before it was written.

Krishna is the hero in Mahabharata (a great epic) and the whole war has been created to prove his supremacy.

In Mahabharata Pandavas (five brothers) fought against their cousins Kauravas in the battle of Kurukshetra and won the war with the help of Krishna. Pandavas were married to a single woman called Draupadi. This concept of five brothers marrying a single woman has been criticized throughout the history but this was intentionally misinterpreted to hide the actual meaning. I would like to shed some light here. First consider who the five brothers are

1. Yudhishthira
2. Bhima
3. Arjuna
4. Nakula
5. Sahadeva

Yudhishthira also called as Dharmaraja, the eldest of all was known for his righteousness. He never deviates from moral and justice. Bhima was known for his strength, aggressiveness and valour. Arjuna was known for his skills in archery. Nakula was known for his beauty and Sahadeva was an introvert known for his wisdom. Both Nakula and Sahadeva were twin brothers. All the five brothers were married to Draupadi. She was the Princess of Panchala kingdom. But among the five brothers, Arjuna was the one who participated in Draupadi's Swayamwara, a kind of royal wedding ceremony, where kings from all around the world were invited to showcase their skills in order to impress the princess. Arjuna impressed Draupadi and also the rest of the royal guest gathered in the swayamwara with his archery skills and married Draupadi. When he took Draupadi to his mother Kunti to introduce her, kunti who was in prayer heard Arjuna's voice and told him to share it among his brothers like the way they usually do. This is how Draupadi has become the single wife of five brothers.

This incident has been taken literally without understanding the significance of the characters and their characteristics. Let's look at the hidden truth behind this story.

Arjuna was known for his archery skills, which needs tremendous concentration, focus and sharpness. We have already seen that Vishnu holds his weapon (chakra) in the right hand which represents the cochlea of the right ear to show the sharpness of right ear over the left ear. Among all the five senses only ear has the capability to concentrate intensively. If one wants to totally concentrate on something, then one closes his eyes and listens through ears. People who are good at listening are highly intellectual in nature and have good memory. Also, we have seen in last chapter that sound is Knowledge; Draupadi is knowledge which enters through ears and takes control of all other senses. So Draupadi (sound) entered through Arjuna (ear) and has been shared by other four brothers (senses).

Yudhishthira is known for his righteousness (Dharma). How a man delivers Dharma (justice)? Through his mouth by speaking, so Yudhishthira is mouth. Next Bhima who was known for his strength and Gluttony is the body (touch). Nakula who was known for his beauty represents eyes because eyes (vision) are the most beautiful among all the senses. Finally

Nakula who was said to be an introvert and known for his wisdom is nose (smell). By smelling one can sense and avoid the danger. Especially when we are doubtful about any food item, first we smell it to confirm whether it is still edible or not. Also any kind of danger like fire or any explosion will be first detected by smelling the smoke. So smelling is considered as an inherent wisdom. Arjuna (ears) brought Draupadi (knowledge) and it has been shared by Dharma (mouth), Bhima (body), Nakula (eyes) and Sahadeva (nose). This is how knowledge (Draupadi) has become the wife of five brothers (Pandavas). It is just to show the arrival of knowledge and development of mind (sixth sense). Also they have indirectly conveyed the way senses develops in a child, through the order of the pancha pandavas. According to vedic people, taste (mouth) is the first sense to develop completely, followed by touch (body) and then hearing (ear) and finally vision (eyes) and nose (smell) develops simultaneously. Among the pandavas, Arjuna is the dearest one to Draupadi because sound (Draupadi) enters through ears (Arjuna).

In another incident Pandavas lose everything to Kauravas in the game of dice (Gambling). Yudhishthira the eldest brother likes gambling, which is very contradictory because how a righteous person who always stands for justice can involve in gambling. But that's what happens with tongue. A single unwanted word, loose tongue is enough to spoil one's own reputation. So Dharma with his loose tongue lost his kingdom and his brothers to Shakuni (Kaurava's maternal uncle). Shakuni is another mastermind known for his cunningness in the Kaurava's group. He provoked Yudhishthira to play one last game by betting Draupadi to recover all his losses. Allured by Shakuni's offer, Yudhishthira played but lost Draupadi to Kauravas. Initially Yudhishthira lost all his possessions which he has earned through mind and finally lost mind also to another illusionist Shakuni who was much cleverer mind than Draupadi. After winning Draupadi, Kauravas decided to disrobe Draupadi in front of everyone to dishonour Pandavas. This normally happens when one's ego (mind) has been proved incapable then one starts feeling low and defeated. Stripping the saree (cloth) is meant to denote peeling-off the layers of mind. Once all the layers of the mind are removed then it becomes clear that mind is an illusion. This is how one attains Nirvana because unless one feels as "I know nothing", Nirvana is not possible. So it has been shown as kauravas disrobing the saree (cloth) of Draupadi but she has been saved by the god of mind (source of all knowledge) Krishna. Krishna gave her unlimited saree, means his knowledge and saved Draupadi.

After this incident, Pandavas understood that they can't win the war against Kauravas with their limited knowledge (Draupadi). So Pandavas took shelter under Krishna (God of Knowledge). They fought the war as per Krishna's guidance and they won the war. Pandavas won the battle only because of the cleverness and intelligence of Krishna (mind). Let's take a look at {Fig.44} one of the most common representations of Krishna as a charioteer driving four horses with Arjuna sitting behind in the war of Kurukshetra. These four horses represent the four senses (taste, touch, vision and smell) and Arjuna is the fifth sense ears and Krishna is the Sixth sense God of knowledge (mind). Krishna has been shown very close to Arjuna among all other pandavas because Krishna is the sound/knowledge which enters through the ears. So there is always a special relationship between sound and ear. This is the actual reason behind the bonding between Arjuna and Krishna. Krishna has chosen Arjuna to deliver the Bagavat Gita for the same reason and even in Bagavat Gita he mentioned Arjuna as his dear friend, so Krishna has transferred all his knowledge to Arjuna.

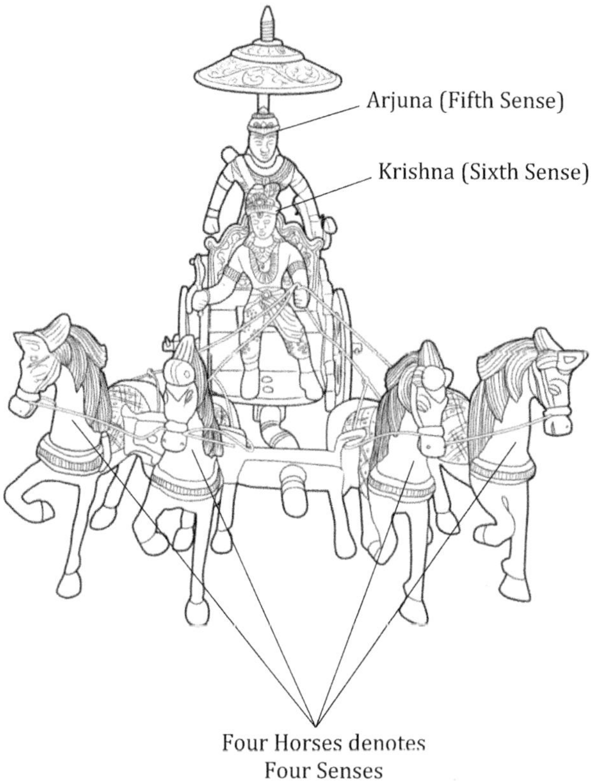

Fig.44 Krishna and Arjuna in Battle of Kurukshetra

I call it knowledge because mind can only give knowledge of liberation not actual liberation. God (Brahman) gives salvation and never knowledge of liberation to anyone. Whoever attained liberation tried to convey it to others through words and later it has become knowledge. Because Truth is an experience and it remains as an experience forever. It can't be explained by language or philosophy which is man–made illusions. No one can attain salvation by reading a certain philosophy or scriptures.

"By reading about Truth one can become a scholar but to experience it, to become a part of it, to dissolve and merge with it, one must unlearn whatever one has learned about it. There is no other way".

So through Bagavat Gita, Vaishnavism (Aryans) has tried to establish their supremacy over the consciousness (Shiva) by declaring Krishna (mind) as the eternal soul dwelling in all the living entity. This is the biggest lie ever told in the history of mankind that mind declaring itself as soul and Supreme Being. As we have clearly seen, what the incarnations are and who Krishna is but this truth has been intentionally hidden for last 25 centuries and projected Krishna (mind) as a God (Supreme Being). One can refer any pictures of the past times of Krishna and can easily relate with the organs inside the ears. The authorities who had written stories and drawn those pictures clearly knew that Krishna is a mind (sound) but their one and only motive was to establish their supremacy over other gods in Hinduism. By adding so many layers of stories, they have created a great drama with a blind faith that no one would be able to discover the actual meaning behind.

This is how people started claiming one god greater than other by creating so many stories and this tradition has been transferred from one generation to another for so many centuries. But all those people who know the actual reasons and meanings for these stories has hidden it and intentionally projected mind as god. They created fear among people by depicting mind as god with four hands holding different weapons in each hand and by telling that these gods are living in far away eternal planets and it's impossible to reach those planets within this lifetime. They brain washed the people by conditioning that only by worshipping the mind one could be free from Karma. One must pray to the god (mind) throughout their life so that one will attain the abode of the particular god after death and could live with the god in the eternal world. These fake dreams which were created by the Aryans, nomadic pastoral people who migrated from central Asia into Indian sub-continent approx. in 1700 BC (Avari, 2007) has been injected into the innocent people's mind who are searching for deeper meaning of life (Truth) and they have been made into slaves for rest of their life. These innocent people start doing crazy things in the name of following religious principles.

This is how the tradition of dominating people using the name of God existing in Hinduism for thousands of years. The innocent people who are following these authorities have wasted and are wasting their whole life living with these cheap dreams. People must awake from the dream of going to other planets, which has been told by someone who himself has no idea of what happens after death. These are the sects who have successors for thousands of years who claim that they are the direct representatives of the God and one has to receive the knowledge of God only through them. They call it as a perfect knowledge because it is coming from the authorities. What they are calling as knowledge is the neuroscience of how mind develops in a man which has been encrypted as a story, which they have created some thousands of years ago. Before the conception of proverbs like ***'Knowledge is power'*** and '***Pen is mightier than sword'***, these authorities actually knew it and have applied it over the people. Sad part is if they would have shared this knowledge with rest of the world, so many neurological disorders would have been identified in the early childhood and treated properly, which would have saved so many precious lives in the last 20 centuries because the western world has started studying the inner ear and its functions only in the middle of the 16th century. It took almost 3 centuries for them to completely understand and discover how the sound waves travel through the ear and processed within the cochlea based on the frequency and reaches brain (Van De Water, 2012).

The authorities also have cleverly carried forward the story to the future and instilled fear among the innocent people by creating Kalki {Fig.45} the last incarnation of Vishnu.

Fig.45 Kalki as Tenth Avatar

They told that when irreligiousness dominates the world he will appear and save the religion and the world. What they are talking about religion and saving religion is to save the Vedas (knowledge). So where the knowledge comes from; mind (Vishnu). There is no meaning for this Kalki avatar because in reality there is no future or past it is always eternal now. By projecting that someone will come in future, they have ensured their authority over the religion which they have created, because to know how and when he (Kalki) will come, one has to depend on the authority. This is how mankind has been reduced into slavery by making them to believe and worship their own mind in the name of following religion. These authorities has created fear among the innocent people and made them to believe the stories which were created to depict the organs within the ear as true. They conditioned people's mind that avatar himself has said that if someone worship Vishnu or Krishna in his original form then they will reach eternal planet where he resides on his thousand headed snake and there people can enjoy playing, dancing and decorating him.

By thinking about the form of god and reading about his stories which someone has created one can't go anywhere other than to one's own mind. This is the highest form of slavery. Freedom is when one comes out of the mind, but by making people to worship their own mind the authorities has ensured that no one will ever attain liberation. Krishna himself was a concept which these authorities have created some centuries ago. Also they have introduced the concept of demigods where they have included Shiva in it to suppress Shaivism. As per their theory, demigods work under the supervision of Krishna and they have written so many stories and verses to support their theory. So if one directly worships Krishna then one can surpass all the demigods. Personal god is itself a concept in Hinduism, where again they created so many sub-divisions and made it very complicated, so that no one can understand it and naturally people has to depend on the authority. Everything is a pure mind game, well executed to trap the people within their mind by telling the stories again and again and make them to believe all the stories as reality and these innocent people are wasting their life without any slightest experience of Truth. If these people would have practised proper meditation they would have attained liberation. These authorities have first introduced the mind as God (Vishnu) and then through his incarnations they have cleverly introduced the Varna (caste) system. They have reserved the upper caste householder priest (Brahmin) for themselves and divided the indigenous people into three classes which are Kshatriya (warriors), Vaisyas (traders) and Sudras (workers). Those who didn't fall into these three castes mostly tribals are called as untouchables (outcaste). The kind of pain and discrimination which the lower caste people (sudras) and outcaste (untouchables) have undergone in the last 20 centuries is unimaginable. These Aryan authorities have hidden their ugly faces behind the mask of god and systematically ruled the country in the name of religion. Contrary to the popular belief that the caste system was strongly enforced only during the British rule to segregate people into smaller groups for colonisation, recent genetics study clearly reveals the fact that strong practise of endogamy (marrying within the same caste) exists in India for thousands of years (Reich, 2018).

Religion is to know who you are, which is not possible unless one stops worshipping one's mind. But these authorities has convinced with all the imaginary stories that by worshipping one's own mind, means by thinking about particular form of god in their mind one will reach higher planets after death. This is totally opposite to the core of Hinduism. Core of Hinduism is attaining liberation (Moksha, Mukthi) while living. This is possible by realizing the Brahman (cosmic consciousness) which is also residing inside everyone as a soul. When one realizes one's Self (Atman), one also experiences the Brahman in everything and everywhere. But this Brahman realization has been portrayed as impersonalist theory and who realized their inner Self are labelled as impersonalist. Core of Hinduism is impersonal and all other personal gods were introduced later with the aim to create authority over the people. As I have mentioned earlier that God can't be a knowledge because God is an experience and it remains as an experience as along as man exists.

"As long as one believes in someone's concept of god, there is no possibility of experiencing the one who is eternally shining in one's being".

8 Hinduism and Buddhism

In the last few chapters we have seen who are the Trinity Gods and the significance behind their representation and the order of Trinity. Also how the different sects in Hinduism has created their own story about the gods which they follow in order to overtake the position of Supreme Being (Brahman). Now I would like to shed some light on Buddhism. I hope that most of the people might have read about the story of Gautama Siddhartha or Buddha (the awakened one), for those who doesn't know I would like to explain it briefly.

Siddhartha who was born to a Hindu king was informed immediately by the royal astrologers that there is a high possibility for his son to turn either into a great king or a great saint. Feared of his son turning into a saint, the king ensured that his son remains within the palace complex and has provided him with all the pleasures of the world right from his childhood to make him unaware about the truth of the real world. But how long one would get involved in worldly pleasures, definitely one will get bored after sometime. So Siddhartha thought of stepping out of the palace with the help of palace guard to visit the outside world. These visits have totally changed his perception about the world he has imagined. On his first visit he saw an old man struggling to walk and in second visit he has seen a man affected by some disease and then in his third visit he saw the corpse of the dead man carried by others. First time in his life, he came to know that every human being falls sick then gradually becomes old and die. He understood that life is full of suffering and no one can escape from this cycle. In his fourth visit he has seen an ascetic with a begging bowl who has renounced everything to encounter the reality. This made him to enquire about what life is. Why it is a series of suffering. As he has seen the peaks of worldly pleasures right from his childhood, it became easy for him to renounce everything without any second thought to find the most important question in life 'Who am I'? He decided to find the answer by himself and rigorously practised different fasting and meditation methods for seven years, but nothing worked. Tired of searching for Truth, he dropped the search and totally relaxed under the Bodhi tree, at that moment the magic happened. Siddhartha became Buddha (the Enlightened one).

He realized that as long as one thinks, one identifies oneself with the ego, one will keep suffering. The moment one separates oneself from the mind (the ego), it becomes clear that man is pure consciousness, awareness, not a doer but a watcher unaffected by external circumstances. Whoever attains one's natural state will be full of love and compassion. So out of compassion he wanted to share his wisdom to others so that they can also realise themselves and put an end to the series of suffering. During that time, people have gone too much into Vedic rituals and sacrifices without understanding the nature of the impersonal god. People were not able to accept what he was telling, because people were already conditioned to worship Vedic gods and believed and lived in their fantasy stories. So people didn't understand him. Some higher caste people who were following the traditional authorities might have understood about what he was talking, but by accepting him they were afraid of losing their jobs. Since they have established the tradition of authority of God over thousands of years, they didn't want to lose their position as a dominating authority among the people.

Buddha realized that if he introduces the concept of God, then definitely after some time people will cling again to that concept instead of knowing the reality. So he decided to remove the concept of God completely and told that the existence is nothingness (emptiness) and this same nothingness is inside everyone. We have already seen that how mind develops and how it makes us unaware of our nature. This mind creates a false identity of self which is totally based on the knowledge one has received and learned from others. If one removes everything that has been added to him right from the childhood then what remains is pure consciousness which is nothingness. But only this nothingness can make the man complete. To realize this that 'I am nothing' is the path of nirvana (Enlightenment) and he called it as end of suffering. He realized that the main problem is the knowledge of God (Vedas) which has been kept as a secret within the Vedic people (Aryans) and used as medium to control the large group of indigenous people. Buddha clearly understood that Vedas were mind-born, so he questioned the authority of Vedic religion and revolted against the Vedic rituals and sacrifices. Infact he told people to disregard the Vedas. This has been received as a great threat to the hierarchy who were claiming authority over Vedas (knowledge). So the authorities had introduced Puranas (mythological stories) after the disappearance of Buddha in order to revive the Vedic religion, later they had very cleverly told that Buddha himself was an avatar of Vishnu (mind). By including Buddha under the avatars of Vishnu, they have suppressed Buddhism. They have played a psychological game by saying that the scriptures recommend worshipping Buddha in other forms of Vishnu and it is the easiest way to attain salvation than the path of Nirvana. Even though Buddhism was born in India it is not very widely practised in India because of the conflict of interest but extensively followed in all East Asian countries. Actually Buddha is the one who has realised that 'I am not the mind' (no mind) where as Vishnu is the mind. In no way Buddha could be considered as an avatar of Vishnu. We have clearly seen what the avatars means and the actual reason behind them.

Even after careful consideration and introduction of nothingness, after the disappearance of Buddha, people again followed the same old pattern of mind. People created so many stories of Buddha and projected Buddha as god and started worshipping him and reading Buddhist scriptures. People always have the notion that more the scriptures, more the knowledge and stronger the foundation of religion. That's how the mind thinks. Later Buddhism started developing and followed with the same old tradition of reading scriptures and mantras which was the worst night mare that Buddha never wanted to happen.

Five centuries after the disappearance of Buddha, there arrived Bodhidharma, a south Indian king who has practised meditation and attained enlightenment. He was instructed by his master to travel to China. He went to China and he was surprised to see that Buddhist monasteries were following the same old tradition of reading scriptures instead of meditating. He revolutionized Buddhism and told to throw away the scriptures and live with awareness. He was very clear that until one carries the teachings of Buddha on his head, one can never become a Buddha. He told clearly,

"The ultimate truth is beyond words because words are illusions".

Later this practice of living with awareness has become a part of Buddhism called Zen. Not thinking about anything is Zen. It can be walking, eating, washing etc. This is the real religiousness. Zen doesn't talk about philosophy rather it is unlearning all kinds of philosophy which one has learned and see the things as it is, that is reality. Man needs to live with awareness, alertness. One who lives with awareness never commits any crime; he will not be threat to anyone. Only those who live in unawareness, who identifies with their mind and obeys the orders of the mind, are the one who are carried away by desires and acts unconsciously and hurt others in order to fulfill their temporary wants.

Nirvana which is the core of Buddhism was also there in Hinduism long back. As I have described earlier that Shiva (God of destroyer) who represents man's attainment of liberation is nothing but Nirvana. So he is depicted as a renounced and he is called as destroyer because he destroys all the dreams, all the illusions that one carries on his head and shows the reality. We have also seen that Lord Karthikeya (Sixth sense) after feeling defeated by his brother God Ganesha renounced everything and stood naked in Palani hills to know himself. Nirvana, Mukthi, Samadhi, Liberation, Salvation all means the same "to know oneself" is the core of Hinduism. Since people have been heavily conditioned for so many centuries to worship the deities they have fallen unconscious and were unable to recognize the truth behind these stories.

So in Buddhism, to avoid the concept of god they have used emptiness instead of consciousness or Self as in Hinduism. And instead of Brahman (Supreme Being) they used the same emptiness to represent existence. This is the only difference between Hinduism and Buddhism.

So we can see from multiple incidents that the essence of Hinduism and Buddhism are basically one and same but Buddhism has become a separate religion because of non acceptance of higher religious authorities in Hinduism.

"Life becomes meaningful when one understands the meaninglessness of words".

9 Mind a Time Machine

In the last few chapters we have seen what actually Hinduism means and how it has depicted the evolution of man from Body, Mind and Consciousness as three different Gods (Brahma, Vishnu and Shiva) and how it has assigned those gods with different roles as creator, preserver and destroyer and the significance behind it. Also we have seen the core similarity between Hinduism and Buddhism. In both the religions, realization of the Self, going beyond the mind and merging with the source is considered as enlightenment or liberation. Buddhism called the existence as nothingness but Hinduism called it as Supreme Being (Brahman), source of everything. It is formless but it expresses itself in different forms. All other living organisms are connected with this Supreme Being except man, that's how other beings respond to natural calamities. They didn't develop any advanced equipments or technology but they all are connected to the source. They respond instinctively which is the actual wisdom because they always live in now moment but we always live only in past and future except the present. Mankind has separated itself from the source by identifying with the sixth sense. Every child arrives as a pure consciousness when it is born and once it starts naming objects around it the sixth sense develops and it forgets its original nature by identifying with the sixth sense (mind). As we have seen from the Namam Symbol on Vishnu's forehead, how the sixth sense closes one's wisdom eye and makes one ignorant of the Self. Out of the sixth sense we have invented everything right from wheel, language to mathematics and time.

We invented time for our reference, to keep the events in order, to bring the past and future into our control (mind). Based on the presence and absence of sunlight we called it as day and night. Later we calculated time by fixing certain reference on earth and its position with respect to the sun and moon and formulated time from nanoseconds to light year and inventing further. All these calculations were made for our intellectual understanding and are not real. Existence is continuously changing in the eternal now and our whole life in the planet is just a tiny fraction of the change. But we have built another world around us with our intellectual capability and started living in a totally artificial world without knowing the reality. Now we are trying to explore the existence (our source) through our intellect which is impossible, because our intellect explores with concepts which we have developed ourselves by observing the universe for thousands of years. All these knowledge made us to look at objects and analyse it through the mind and not as it is. That's where the knowledge fails.

It is a simple fact that the Supreme Being (Brahman) is ever-present reality and our universe and other galaxies were born out of it and it is the one which is residing as a life energy (soul, Self) inside every living organism. Every being is connected to it but only those who attained enlightenment were able to hear and experience it. Our science has classified electromagnetic spectrum based on our intellectual observation right from radio waves, microwaves, infrared, visible light, ultraviolet, X-rays, and gamma rays but the sound of the Supreme Being doesn't fit into any of these range. How did we leave the sound of the Brahman and why no equipment is able to detect it which is present throughout our space and beyond? This clearly shows that cosmic consciousness (Brahman) is beyond our intellect and we have created our material world based on our own theories through which we can't quantify the existence. The one and only way to experience the Brahman (source) is by surrendering. Surrendering doesn't mean kneeling or bowing down rather it means to surrender one's intellect, 'I' the ego. If one's ego dissolves, Truth happens immediately. Even after dropping our intellect we can only experience the Truth but we can't explore it. It always remains as an un-explorable. We can just become part of it and remain in that cosmic bliss forever.

As Socrates told ***"To know thyself is the beginning of wisdom"*** and ***"The only true wisdom is in knowing, you know nothing"***. He meant, by looking through our mind (knowledge) one becomes an ignorant, one fails to look at reality. Unless one drops all his knowledge and come to an understanding that I know nothing and look literally with a naked eye only then one can live in reality which is wisdom. This is why Hinduism has depicted Shiva with his wisdom eye in the middle of the fore head. Naturally everyone arrives with a wisdom eye opened but it closes as soon as the knowledge enters. This is what Jesus mentioned as ***"unless you change and become like a little child, you will never enter into the kingdom of heaven"***. We are living and looking at the world with so many concepts which we have developed ourselves. Time is one of those concepts. In reality there is no time, time is an illusion. It is always eternal now. But our whole life has been designed to live with reference to time. The moment a baby arrives, we notice the time, date and year and it remains as a reference to calculate how old someone is. So whenever someone asks you about your age, you need to remember the particular year and it gives the feeling of getting old and also you observe the bodily changes with respect to that year of birth and call ourselves as young, adult, old and dead. In existence every organisms appears and disappears but they don't calculate their age. We because of our intellectual capability started naming every object around us and also ourselves with respect to our appearance and changes, because we wanted to bring everything into our known world into our intellect. We believe that by creating theories we can understand the naturally occurring phenomenon. We feel at ease when we bring the unknown things into our known world by studying and naming them with different hypothesis and theories. Over so many thousands of years we have developed this knowledge about ourselves and about other living and non-living organisms around us. With all this knowledge, we have defined a particular pattern for our life. We have created so many rules to be followed during every step of our life and defined so many milestones to be completed within certain age in order to fit into the society as a successful person. We have made a blue print for how a man has to live right from his birth to death and there are some religious people who believe in next life, even perform rituals and sacrifices to get a better life or to go to higher planets in next birth. So while living we waste our whole life in thinking and accomplishing about certain targets or goals in the future. We always think and imagine about the future and forget to live in the present which is actual living.

Time itself is a concept which we have created. We are also trying to explore other sub-concepts like time travel. There are fantasy concepts like time machine which can take one from the present to certain year in the past and also it has the capability to take one to particular year in the future. So that one can go to the future and see one's life and come back to the present and can change certain events in the present to avoid certain events happening in the future. There were so many movies which has been made based on this concept of travelling to past and future. But all this concepts will remain as concepts forever, for the simple reason there is no time. It is always eternal now. But Man himself is a time machine because we have been so deeply conditioned ourselves with the concept of time for so many centuries which is the foundation of mind. Mind is your time machine. It keeps thinking continuously without break. It wouldn't stop even while sleeping; it projects the same thoughts in the name of dreams. About what it thinks? It can't think about the present. So it has to think about the past and future which are illusions, because past has already gone and it is impossible to change it and future is uncertain no one knows what it would be. So mind creates all combination of thoughts and keeps you always unconscious of the present and takes away your life.

***"You are not the thinker but the thinker is making you unaware of your nature by thinking continuously*"**.

I call mind is a time machine because mind can take you to the past, to whatever year or incident which you remember; you can visit your sweet or bad memories. Also if some unpleasant incident has happened in the past which is still hurting you in the present, you can always revisit that incident and imagine or replace it with a pleasant moment and feel yourself at ease. Similarly mind can easily take you to the future, you can also go to whichever year you want and imagine whatever you wanted to be in the future and enjoy the way you wanted at least in your dreams.

We have created the concept of time and time travel based on our intellectual capability to dream about the past and future. We started thinking that the time travel could be a possibility and so many calculations are going on in order to make it into a reality. But the past and future exists only in the mind and not in reality. Beyond the mind time doesn't exist, man enters into timeless zone of eternal now. So when one starts living in the present with complete awareness there wouldn't be any thoughts about the past events, which is tremendous relief from suffering. Also the fear of future, fear of uncertainty the biggest fear of mankind would not be there if one lives intensely in the present. Mind creates fear that's how it survives.

"Mind is nothing more than a fear manufacturing factory".

Because we have taken our life for granted and have made so many commitments in future, we are always made to live in the future through our thoughts. These future oriented thoughts has been implanted into child's mind right from their school in the name of ambition and setting role model in certain field like whom they wanted to become. That's how we train the kids to dream about future and take away their happiness. Happiness is simply being oneself, its one's original nature. One doesn't need to become anyone or acquire anything in order to become happy. All these goals and motivations are made just to survive in this society and nothing less.

By making you unaware of your nature, you have been conditioned to accept the idea that happiness is in becoming a celebrity or a millionaire. Everyone has been made to believe that the purpose of the life is to become someone recognized by the society. Even those who have become celebrity or achieved their dream are also not satisfied with their life and are regretting for wasting so many years of their precious life to achieve the worthless goals and still feeling empty and searching for happiness. If you are searching for power, wealth or knowledge you can search outside but if you believe that by acquiring power, wealth and knowledge you become happy, it's totally wrong calculation and that's how the majority of the people think. It doesn't matter whichever position one holds or whatever wealth or knowledge one has acquired, one can never feel complete without knowing the Self because whatever one has become or acquired is a man-made illusion.

As Jesus said ***"The kingdom of heaven is within you",*** everything is within you already. You are blessed with happiness in your being; you have the capability to experience the infinite existence but as long as you search outside you are simply wasting your life.

"Happiness, peace, Truth or god whatever the name one gives to eternity. It's within you; don't waste life in searching outside".

10 Inner Transformation

Life which we are living now has become more of artificial than original. Throughout our life we are chasing for the things which we don't have and waste our whole life without getting satisfied with the things we have already acquired after years of chasing.

We always crave for more, without realizing the value of what we already have, but life has its own way of teaching to show what is really important.

People are continuously bombarded with so many ideas about new products and technology and everyone is always looking to change certain things in their life because they are not happy or bored with their old life style. But people forget to notice that the same boredom keeps repeating day after day, month after month, year after year, the same dissatisfaction with life, same longing for happiness. Majority of the people believe that after acquiring certain amount of money or after buying certain product they can live happily forever. But after acquiring what they desired for, they realize that there is no happiness in it and again they waste their life in searching for something else. That's how the whole world is moving.

In India there is a wide spread thought that a girl must have fair complexion which has been implanted by the main stream media. Through so many years of beauty product commercials they have conditioned the people's mind with this idea. But whatever the beauty product one uses, it cannot change the complexion which one has got by birth which comes from one's parents and their ancestors. Also it depends on which region of the country they have lived and climatic condition prevailed there. This can't be changed and doesn't need to be changed because it's their natural body tone but because of wide spread advertisement about fair complexion; girls with dark complexion were forced to change their skin tone in order to make them fit into the society, in order to get married and even to get a job in MNC's. They were made to feel themselves inferior because of their skin complexion. No bridegroom is ready to marry them and there were also cases of suicide. We can't blame anyone directly for this situation but people's mind has been heavily conditioned for the past three decades to believe that fairer skin is superior to dark complexion through advertisements and it is showing its effects now. This is just an example to show how we have been conditioned to believe certain things as reality which is not.

Everyone wants to change into someone else in order to get accepted by the society and to become happy. They are not ready to accept themselves as they are. This is the root cause of suffering in life.

"There is no greater sin than imitating and following others out of fear rather than being one's authentic Self".

When one accepts oneself completely as how one has been by nature physically, intellectually then one's outlook of life changes significantly. As more the time we spent on changing ourselves we forget who we are originally. The problem is that we think ourselves as the body and mind and we spend much time in changing our external appearances as per the current trend and also adapt our mind to current lifestyle in society. There is nothing wrong in it and both (body and mind) are absolutely fine but both (body and mind) are part of you but not the actual you. Your mind always believes that everyone is moving ahead of you, so you also need to follow it otherwise you will miss the train. This has been happening ever since the establishment of society. You have been conditioned to follow a particular pattern during different phases of life. You have been given a blue print of education, career, family, children and where to reach after 10 years, 40 years, after retirement and also after death. This blue print assures you wealth but misses the most fundamental desire of mankind, to be happy. Happiness wouldn't come by running after something rather it comes when one realizes that there is no need to run. Everyone is running because of their commitments which they had made out of their ignorance by following someone. From the childhood we have been conditioned to become better and smarter than our friends and neighbours. This smartness is polished name given to cunningness. This thought of being better than others has been sown as a seed in every child's mind right from the kindergarten. Later this seed grows into an ugly tree, bearing poisonous fruits like anger, aggression, hatred, jealously and vengeance among us. Everyone is capable of transforming themselves into beautiful sculpture but with this idea of being smarter than other we literally start seeing each other as a competitor. In order to win the competition naturally we start hiding things from each other and give false information. This is the typical behaviour of mind. It can do anything for its survival. Majority of the people are carrying the same kind of thought to become better and smarter than others. This illusionary idea of to be ahead of the crowd, definitely makes one to think a lot, one needs to analyse so many factors and probability. All these consume so much of life energy, which literally leads to frustration and suffering. This is how man loses his happiness as he starts growing older. He will be always thinking and worrying about the future which takes one away from the present.

"By thinking, one chooses to remain in hell and by living one re-enters heaven".

As Socrates told ***"An unexamined life is not worth living".***

Unless one finds the unchangeable within oneself, one can't live at peace because of continuous hankering of mind to chase one after another. To put an end to life long suffering, one has to understand 'who am I'? One has to begin the journey of inner transformation. Initially one can start with reading about the experiences of enlightened people which can help in giving glimpse of the reality. But it is impossible to find the direct answer anywhere because this question can't be answered by anyone. It has to come as an experience directly from the Truth because the experience of the state of thoughtlessness can't be conveyed through thoughts. Language which was born out of limited intelligence of human mind doesn't possess the essence to capture the state of mindlessness. In reality there is no name for any object but we have named it in order to create a common platform to communicate with each other which we call as language. But the moment you name an object it simply means you are different from the object, because of this dualistic nature it is impossible to convey the Truth through language. There are many Zen monks who never wrote any book because of the same reason. There is a beautiful Zen saying about it,

"Words are the fog one has to see through".

So this search for truth has to go beyond books and should be an individual journey, someone can help in re-conditioning you, remove your mental constraints and show the path but no one can take you along the path. The path remains always open but it has to be travelled alone. To know oneself one needs to spend much time with oneself in silence. One has to watch oneself. Not thinking about anything is meditation. One can sit in a lotus posture (better one) because this is how Shiva, the liberated one has been depicted. If there is any problem in sitting straight then one can sit in any other position which one feels comfortable and close one's eyes and meditate in silence without thinking about anything. One can follow this simple meditation without any expectations. This has to be done only to relax oneself from the thoughts. To take a break from mind's non-stop screening, to be in peace for sometime. Another important thing is that one should not create positive thoughts or imagine a person or image of god while observing silence. There shouldn't be any time line or target because it can bring the mind into the picture as I told; time is the foundation of the mind. If mind enters, it can create all imaginations of feeling peace and enlightenment. So be watchful. You are just going to watch yourself, let the thoughts come and go like the clouds passing over the sky. If one follows this regularly then gradually one can see a difference in one's life, because when one consciously starts watching oneself, at some point one starts experiencing brief interval between thoughts which creates a clear difference between the mind and Self. Initially it can be experienced for few minutes but it will keep increasing as you travel along the path. Then, there arises an awareness which always remains with you forever. You wouldn't identify you with your mind anymore. You know that you are pure consciousness which is illuminating the body. You become a pure witness of your own Self. One becomes Shiva. As I mentioned earlier that becoming Shiva is like rebirth, because you have totally detached yourself from the mind and understood clearly that you are not the mind. You have attained your original nature which is eternal happiness, thoughtlessness. There is no greater thing than this that can happen in one's life. You can live among the crowd and you can carry on your everyday activities but you clearly know what reality is and you wouldn't consider mind's ideas and get trapped in it out of ignorance. This is wisdom. Knowing oneself is actual wisdom.

You would not differentiate anything and you will accept things as they are. You understand that happiness is in your nature and it doesn't depend on anyone or anything. You know that you are immortal. As your ego melts and dissolves into the existence, you understand that you are not separate but part of existence (Brahman). You have saved yourself from Karmas (reactions from past actions) and you remain in pure bliss every moment. You know that all living beings are one and the same. With this awareness you lead the life unaffected by external circumstances. There wouldn't be any questions anymore because the questioner has already disappeared. You shower peace and compassion to everyone around you. You wouldn't compare yourself with anyone anymore. You know that everyone is unique and start accepting them as they are. You stop running after temporary fame, wealth and pleasure but at the same time you can perform your daily work uninterrupted by the results. This is the way of life. This is religion. This happens when you change your identity from mind to inner Self. You start enjoying yourself and also with people around, nothing will disturb you. You can feel the completeness of life within you. You realise that nothing is missing or to be added in your life in order to be complete. You have attained oneness. You have lost your ego into the infinite and you have become part of the infinite. This transformation can happen only through meditation.

"Only the mind travels back and forth into past and future, neither the body nor the Self".

11 Humanity is One

In the previous chapter I discussed about the inner transformation of one's identity from mind to no mind and attain one's original nature which is eternal bliss with an example of god Shiva. I have explained about Hinduism and its hidden truth, to reveal the actual meaning of the gods and to remind the core philosophy of Hinduism "the oneness of all beings". I used the same example of god Shiva which is easier to understand the nature of one who has attained his inner peace. Here, I want to convey that our original nature is peace and happiness; all the religions have been originated to help us to understand who we are. Most of their core philosophy will be the same. As mankind has migrated and settled in various regions of the planet according to their personal preferences and for safety reasons, every group has created their own way of worshipping and practises to attain the truth. But the truth which all the religions are talking about is always one and the same, because humanity is one so the truth must be one. We all have come from one source, we are pure consciousness but we have been conditioned for so many centuries based on our location of birth to believe that only our religion and practises are the only truth and everything else is false.

Religion is an instrument through which one can know his original nature. Instead of using religion as a vehicle to transcend ourselves into eternal spiritual being, we are used by the religion. This has been happening for so many centuries. Our mind has been conditioned to believe certain traditions and rules based on the religion we follow, which prevents us from accepting other religions as the way they are. Even though people are ready to accept each other, the authorities of the religion are not allowing them. These authorities, who were afraid of losing their share of population, always create hatred towards other religions and people. Since we are unconscious and were trained to follow the crowd from the childhood, we are unable to see the reality. Religion has become a political weapon rather than a spiritual path. We have been given a thought that our religion's strength is decreasing and we should be strong enough to fight against others. In fact most of the wars and crimes which are happening around the world are because of religious reasons.

People have been conditioned to such an extent that the immigrants who belong to other religion are increasing in their country and it is their duty to do something to stop those migrant people, otherwise their country which was birth place of certain religion will lose its value after certain years. People start believing these ideas as reality and consider that they have to play a role in order to stop this immigration. These kinds of incidents were taking place because of blind faith; blind following of religion without realising that one has been used by someone for political gains. All this can happen only in unawareness. When one doesn't know the reality then one blindly follows the crowd. Remember one thing that whatever the religion which exists today, which one follows today was not there before 5000 years and we don't know whether it will be there after 5000 years. So before 5000 years who our ancestors were, which religion they followed no one knows then why we need to worry too much about saving our religion and want to become saviour of the religion. We are greater than whatever the religion we follow. We are humanity. We are love and we survive on compassion. This is what religion means. Religion means living with awareness, living with love every moment. Every action which comes out of awareness, out of love, out of consciousness is religiousness. Our whole existence is religious place; don't get deluded by the mind which creates an illusion that only certain place or religion is holy. Main purpose of any religion is to bring humanity together but when the religion itself becomes a source of conflict, creating a boundary among each other then certainly we are moving in a totally wrong destructive direction.

Life is changing; we are not the ones before 5000 years. So much has changed, our lifestyle has changed. We can't stick to the same old philosophies which were made for that time. We must awake to reality. We are given this precious life to live. Live every moment, there is no other purpose of life other than living. No one is here to save any religion. There is no greater achievement for anyone in this lifetime, if he can save himself from the mind. In fact all religions are made up of concepts which one thinks as reality until one identifies oneself with body and mind. Only one's body and mind belongs to certain religion not the Self (consciousness) and man is neither the body nor the mind. Man is an immortal soul residing within the body without any conditioning. It can't be conditioned because it is beyond mind born language. It is an energy (an awareness filled with love) without any memory. So whatever the thought that arises in you is coming from the mind. The mind is not actually you but what you think as you. This identification with mind has to be removed by bringing awareness. Be conscious of every action. Don't act as per the instruction of the mind; try to create a gap by watching the thoughts coming from the mind. There is no good thought or bad thought don't analyse it, when you analyse it by creating another thought to study the previous thought, you have already identified with the mind because all the thoughts come from the mind.

If one starts watching the thoughts, then after sometime naturally one becomes a watcher (witness) and starts living moment to moment instead of referring old thought patterns. One starts living instinctively which is actually wisdom. A conscious being never follows the crowd; one can't be trapped by any kind of conditioning when he starts living with awareness. Nobody belongs to any race, community, religion or nation. But everyone thinks so they become a part of particular religion or nation based on their place of birth. This identification is very dangerous, because it gives a false pride about one's religion or nation which we have created ourselves which is not reality. All these illusions acts as a collective mind (society) which controls the people in particular region with certain set of rules and regulations and the same society creates differences between people living in other parts of the world who belong to other country and religion. Our entire planet is a one place but we have created boundaries by naming it as different countries.

By waging war against each other and proving one greater than other we are living in an imaginary world of the mind. No one can conquer the world, as long as one thinks of conquering the world; he is under the influence of the mind. Throughout the history there were so many incidents of the great rulers who tried to conquer the world, but had been conquered by the death and they left earth with so much grief in their death bed for wasting their whole life to live somewhere in the future moments. All those rulers failed, because they all tried to conquer their own mental projections. Life is a zero sum game; one comes and leaves with empty hands. So understand this fundamental truth and live wisely. The world which you see is just the projection of your inner world and it will keep changing according to the expansion of your knowledge. Earlier, people thought that the world means only the land, so they wasted their life in conquering the land. Now with the expansion of our science and technology and our capability to launch space ship to other planets, every nation is trying to conquer the outer space. We have created most powerful nuclear weapons and deadly viruses which can wipe off the entire human race. A single destructive thought can lead to major damage to life on earth. History keeps repeating itself, but people have fallen asleep and has become totally unaware to recognize the same old pattern of conquering the world is continuing. People have to wake up from this dream to understand the reality.

Existence has given us this liveliest planet with abundance of everything needed for the survival of every living organism. But we in the name of unnecessary competition, greed and false pride among nations and for personal benefits, started destructing our planet's resources very rapidly and now searching for alien life and thinking about migrating to other planets. We need to understand that our body has evolved here for thousands of years and we can't survive in any other planet other than our beautiful earth. This is our home; in order to keep our home at peace, we must remove all our differences and come to common understanding that we are one. Even though we are divided by caste, language, religion, nation etc. the one (soul) which is within everyone is same and the same one is within every living organism. We are not here to compete with each other, we are here with one and only purpose to 'Live'. This is possible only by removing the hatred and sharing the love and compassion among each other. We are here to celebrate our life without disturbing others. We need to live in communion with nature to live a more peaceful life. A universal transformation is required among people living in all corners of the world to accept that we are one, in order to make our lives more beautiful, more peaceful, more playful and more joyful.

"There is only one, the one is in everything and everything is within the one".

Bibliography

1. Avari, B. (2007). *India: The Ancient Past.* Routledge.

2. Blatrix, S., & Mondain, M. (2020, july 13). *Ear.* Retrieved from http://www.neuroreille.com/promenade/english/ear/fear.htm

3. Bryan, K. (1989). Language Prosody and the Right Hemisphere. *Aphasiology , 3* (4), 285-299.

4. Cook, N. D. (2002). Bihemispheric Language : How the Two Hemispheres Colloborate in the Processing of Langauge. *106*, pp. 169-194. Proceedings of British Academy.

5. Friederici, A. D. (2011). The Brain Basis of Language Processing: From Structure to Functions. *Physiological Reviews , 91* (4), 1357-1392.

6. Friederici, A. D., & Alter, K. (2004). Lateralization of Auditory Language Functions: A Dynamic Dual Pathway Model. *Brain and Language , 89* (2), 267-276.

7. Friederici, A. D., Brauer, J., & Lohman, G. (2011). Maturation of the Language Network: From Inter- to Intrahemispheric Connectivities. *Plos One , 6* (6).

8. Gale Sloan Thompson, R. (2015). Sense Organs. In *Understanding Anatomy & Physiology* (2nd ed., pp. 211-214). F. A. Davis Company.

9. Hardy, M. (1938). The Length of the Organ of Corti in Man. *American Journal of Anatomy , 62* (2), 291–311.

Bibliography (Cont.)

10. Hayes, S. H., Ding, D., Salvi, R. J., & Allman, B. L. (2013). Anatomy and Physiology of the External, Middle and Inner Ear. In *Handbook of Clinical Neurophysiology* (Vol. 10, pp. 3-23). Elsevier.

11. Michael-Titus, A., Revest, P., & Shortland, P. (2010). Hearing and Balance: The Auditory and Vestibular Systems. In *The Nervous System* (2nd ed., pp. 141-158). Churchill Livingstone.

12. Nikhilananda, S. (1947). *Self-Knowledge.* Sri Ramakrishna Math.

13. Ocklenburg, S., & Gunturkun, O. (2018). Language and the Left Hemisphere. In *The Lateralized Brain: The Neuroscience and Evolution of Hemispheric Asymmetries* (pp. 87-121). Academic Press.

14. Pujol, R., Nouvian, R., & Lenoir, M. (2016, September 19). *Hair Cells: Overview.* Retrieved from http://www.cochlea.eu/en/hair-cells

15. Rask-Andersen, H., Liu, W., Erixon, E., Kinnefors, A., Pfaller, K., Schrott-Fischer, A., et al. (2012). Human Cochlea: Anatomical Characteristics and their Relevance for Cochlear Implantation. *Anatomical Record , 295* (11), 1791-1811.

16. Reich, D. (2018). The Collision That Formed India. In *Who We Are and How We Got Here* (1 ed., pp. 123-153). Oxford University Press.

Bibliography (Cont.)

17. Sininger, Y. S., & Cone-Wesson, B. (2004). Asymmetric Cochlear Processing Mimics Hemispheric Specialization. *Science* .

18. Van De Water, T. R. (2012). Historical Aspects of Inner Ear Anatomy and Biology that Underlie the Design of Hearing and Balance Prosthetic Devices. *The Anatomical Record* , *295*, 1741-1759.

Printed in Dunstable, United Kingdom

64560425R00090